RADIANT

Radiant

Living as Light in a Dark World

Marian Jordan

PUBLISHING GROUP
Nashville, Tennessee

978-0-8054-4672-2

Published by B&H Publishing Group
Nashville, Tennessee

Dewey Decimal Classification: 248.843
Subject Heading: WOMEN \ CHRISTIAN LIFE \
DISCIPLESHIP

1 2 3 4 5 6 7 8 • 14 13 12 11 10

Dedication
To my precious nieces:
Samantha, Allie, Jenna, and Spencer.
I pray you will love Jesus with all of your hearts
and shine brightly as radiant lights
in the darkness of your generation.

Contents

Arise, shine, for your light has come,
and the glory of the LORD rises upon you.
See, darkness covers the earth
and thick darkness is over the peoples,
but the LORD rises upon you
and his glory appears over you.
Nations will come to your light,
and kings to the brightness of your dawn.

Isaiah 60:1–3 (NIV)

"You are the light of the world.
A city on a hill cannot be hidden."

Matthew 5:14

CHAPTER ONE

A Radiant Woman
Is "in Love" with Jesus

The Glow

Every girl wants to be picked. Singled out. Chosen. Loved.
And when she is, well, that's the stuff fairy tales are
made of:

- Boy meets girl.
- Boy picks girl.
- On one knee.
- With a ring.

And that brings us to this day . . .

Basked in candlelight, the sanctuary is perfectly decorated
and filled with friends and family who have come to celebrate

the joyous union. Amidst the sweet aroma of peonies, gardenias, and lilies, the old familiar sound of Mozart's "Wedding March" is heard. On perfect cue, the church doors creak open, and the guests know the moment they have all been waiting for has arrived.

A hush falls.

Like a trained marching band that pivots in unison, the wedding guests, following the lead of the bride's mother, stand, turn, watch—waiting for their first glimpse of the bride.

Speaking of waiting, from the very first time she heard Cinderella's tale of "happily ever after," the bride began to long for this moment. She just knew that one day her prince would come, sweep her off her feet, and tell her that she is "the one" with whom he wants to spend the rest of his life. One day *she* would be picked. Even when it wasn't cool and when she wouldn't dare confess her heart's true desire out loud . . . still, she hoped.

I believe every little girl rehearses her own version of her fairy-tale moment—that moment when she falls head over heels in love with the man of her dreams. Some keep scrapbooks, and others keep their desires hidden deep in their hearts. Always hoping for "her" day. There is something magical about a wedding that literally captivates the heart of a girl, causing a love affair of the imagination with the idea that one day she will be the bride.

For this bride, her time is *now.* With her arm tucked securely in the nook of her father's and with her heart beating wildly, she steps forward as the church doors open and she is finally revealed.

A million tiny details led to this moment: a first date that led to a "save the date"; hundreds of prayers on her knees that led to his bended knee; dozens of dresses that led to "the dress"; and oodles of alterations, registrations, invitations, contracts, fittings, tastings, and rehearsals—all for her dream wedding.

Looking at her father, she whispers, "I'm ready." And with those words, they step through the door.

The guests inhale deeply as they finally behold her beauty. Perfectly framed in the doorway, she pauses. She wears the classic white dress, and her head is adorned with a cathedral-length veil. Yet, it is not her dress that takes their breath away; it is her face . . . for she is radiant.

Her beauty on this day emanates from a source deep within her soul. She is not beautiful because of a makeup artist's tricks or a hairstylist's skills. No, there is a different quality today, something that is impossible to contain. If this beauty could be bottled, every cosmetic company in the world would clamor for the patent. But it can't be bottled, or produced, for this kind of beauty. Radiance comes from one thing: basking in the glow of love.

Brides are most often described as radiant for a very good reason. It is universally acknowledged that a woman is most beautiful when she is "in love." When basking in the glow of another's love, she feels whole, complete, confident, and adored; her outer expression and countenance emanate from an inner reality. She knows she is loved, and she is head over heels "in love" with her groom.

That, my friends, is radiance.

In Love

At dawn that Sunday, Mary Magdalene slipped into the cold Jerusalem morning. Her destination was the garden where they had buried her Savior. She was the first person to the tomb. The other disciples were too afraid to surface from hiding, but not Mary. She didn't care; she had one person on her mind: Jesus. Putting myself in her shoes, I can imagine what she might have been thinking: *What could the Romans do to me now?* They'd already taken away the one who mattered most to her in the world. As she ran toward the tomb, I can just imagine that her stomach was in knots and that she might have thought back to the first day she saw Him, her Lord.

He entered her village, and her world turned upside down. Everyone had heard of Him, but now she would see the One who many believed was the Messiah—the Savior. Could He be? "Just one glimpse," she told herself. She'd always heard that the Messiah would make all things new—He would heal the sick, give sight to the blind, and free the captives. She did the math and thought, *I've got two out of three working for me. Maybe if I just see Him, my years of torture will end.* She pressed through the crowds, which parted at her presence. No one wanted to associate with such an unclean, crazed woman. No one but Jesus, that is.

All it took was one touch and she was healed. Jesus touched her, and for the first time in her life, she breathed the sweet air of freedom. She believed. "He *is* the Messiah—the Son of the Living God." Revelation brought transformation.

From that moment on, she devoted her life to following her Savior. Words cannot express the love she felt for Him. How can you not love the One who sets you free? How can you not love the One who heals your body, soul, and spirit? How can you not love the One who unconditionally accepts you when all you've known your whole life is rejection?

I can imagine that Mary, weeping as she hurried toward the tomb, sighed and might have thought, He cast seven demons out of me, yet didn't save His own life from crucifixion. I'm living proof that He had the power—why did He submit to such a death? It doesn't seem right.

As Mary neared her destination, she stopped with a fright. The grave . . . the tomb . . . the stone—it was gone! Assuming the worst, she sprinted back to get Peter and John. Gasping for air, she reported the news, "They've taken the Lord, and we don't know where they have put Him!" Upon hearing her information, the two men ran to the tomb.

Mary was right. Jesus was not there. Peter and John found the strangest thing: the stone *was* rolled away, and inside His clothes were neatly folded. Confused, they turned and headed back to join the others. But, not Mary. She stood outside the tomb crying.

The events of the past few days had caught up with her. The flood of grief poured out. With hot tears streaming down her cheeks, she bent over to look inside the tomb and saw two angels seated where Jesus' body had been. The angels asked her, "Woman, why are you crying?" I can imagine that she was likely too overwhelmed with grief to be frightened, so she said, "They have taken my Lord away, and I don't know where they've put Him."

What happened next will be forever branded upon her heart. She turned away from the angels and found a man standing before her. Assuming he was the gardener, she continued on until he said her name, "Mary."

Stopping in mid stride, she spun around to face the one speaking. She knew that voice! That was the voice of the One who had set her free. That was the voice that healed her life. That was the voice that gave her hope to keep living. That was the voice of her Jesus.

"Teacher!" she exclaimed as she flung herself at Him. I can imagine that as she clung to Him, she was probably wondering how to understand His living and breathing presence before her. *Could it be true? Is it really my Lord? How can this be? I watched Him die, but here He is very much alive.*

Loosening her hold on Him, Jesus commissioned her, the woman who was once defeated by demons, to be His voice of victory: "Mary, go tell the others. I am alive!" Obediently, with a heart overflowing with joy, she ran back to the disciples, becoming the first to proclaim the resurrection of her Christ. With a radiant smile, she declared, "I have seen Jesus—He is alive!"

Mary Magdalene loved Jesus with the purest sense of devotion. Affection born out of gratitude, she knew what it meant to receive mercy, forgiveness, healing, and grace. More than that, Mary knew that Jesus loved *her*. After all, it was His love that transformed her from the inside out. Mary models for us a radiant life, one that follows Jesus and serves Jesus in response to His amazing love. She was so "in love" with Him that worshipping, obeying, and adoring Him was the air she breathed.

As we go forward in discovering this thing called radiance—what it is and what it isn't—I want you to keep Mary in the forefront of your mind. She glowed with the passion of a woman enthralled with Jesus.

My testimony is not too different from Mary Magdalene's (without the whole "eyewitness of the resurrection" tidbit, of course). Other than the biggie, I can relate to her on so many levels. Jesus also set me free. Free from insecurities, anxieties, and addictions—powerful enemies that bowed to His name.

Like Mary, I fell head over heels in love with my Savior. How could I not? Forgiveness fuels love's flame. I was whole and healed, something I'd never known before Him. This love drove me, propelled me, to follow after Jesus with my whole heart. And I did. The more I followed Him, the more I loved Him. The more He revealed Himself to me through His Word, the more my life was transformed for His glory. I, too, was enthralled. I couldn't wait to spend time with Him. I was ruined for anything else but Jesus.

Also, like Mary, I was called to proclaim His resurrection. I couldn't wait to tell everyone and anyone about the One who'd set me free—My Messiah! I remember telling a friend one time, "I literally have butterflies when I hear the name of Jesus." Girls, I was a goner.

Love Is a Battlefield

A few nights ago I watched the movie *13 Going on 30* with a friend of mine. That movie never fails to make me laugh. The *Thriller* dance sequence alone makes it a classic. Since I am a child of the 1980s, I can so identify with the awkward-big-bangs-bad-hair-fluorescent-clothing-vibe that the movie portrays.

One of my favorite scenes from this movie is when Jennifer Garner's character turns to her "friends" (the teenage girls living in her building) and admonishes them with these words: "Girls, love is a battlefield." At that point the whole crew breaks out into '80s dance moves with Pat Benatar blaring in the background.

Girls, let's face it, love *is* a battlefield . . . especially our love for Jesus. There is a war raging against it. Satan, the enemy of our souls, despises our pure love and devotion for Christ. He will fight to distract, to divert, and to deter us from anything that deepens our love and affection because he is fully aware that a woman in love with Jesus is dangerously radiant.

Over the years I've experienced this battle. Distractions. Temptations. Enticements. All these lures designed to pull me away from my first love. The reason? Love is the greatest motivator in the world. Many assume that fear is a better one, but I disagree. Consider every drama penned by the hands of men that tell of the lengths that love went to rescue, save, and protect its beloved. Men storm castles, lovers drink poison, soldiers take bullets—all in the name of love.

People overcome fear, they don't overcome love. Satan knows this is true. Better yet, God knows this is true. That is why He said to us, above all else . . . *love Me.*

> One of the teachers of the law came and heard them debating. Noticing that Jesus had given them a good answer, he asked him, "Of all the commandments, which is the most important?"
>
> "The most important one," answered Jesus, "is this: 'Hear, O Israel, the Lord our God, the Lord is one. **Love the Lord your God with all your heart** and with all your soul and with all your mind and with all your strength.'" (Mark 12:28–30, emphasis added)

"If you **love me**, you will obey what I command." (John 14:15, emphasis added)

When they had finished eating, Jesus said to Simon Peter, "Simon son of John, **do you truly love me** more than these?"

"Yes, Lord," he said, "you know that I love you."

Jesus said, "Feed my lambs."

Again Jesus said, "Simon son of John, **do you truly love me?**"

He answered, "Yes, Lord, you know that I love you."

Jesus said, "Take care of my sheep."

The third time he said to him, "Simon son of John, **do you love me?**"

Peter was hurt because Jesus asked him the third time, "Do you love me?"

He said, "Lord, you know all things; you know that I love you."

Jesus said, "Feed my sheep." (John 21:15–17, emphasis added)

Love is central. God knows that if we love Him, we will follow Him, live for Him, obey Him, glorify Him, lay down our lives for Him, lead others to Him—love is that powerful.

One of the "aha moments" of my Christian life was when I realized the connection between loving God and living for

God's glory. God revealed to me the intrinsic connection of the two early on in my relationship with Him. Jesus' words, "if you love me, you will keep my commands," jumped off the pages of my Bible and alerted my heart to its great need: my heart must first love God if I was to obey God.

You see, I knew my own heart well enough to realize that I would give myself fully to whatever I loved the most. Knowing this about myself I prayed a life-changing prayer—one that I still pray every day because I know its power. My prayer is this: *Jesus, give me a heart to love You more than anything else in this world.*

I must testify to what happens in the human heart when we fall in love with Jesus: our desires are transformed. Before I loved Jesus, I lived for myself and for my selfish desires. I did not consider God or His ways.

Then my eyes began to open to the beauty of Jesus and to comprehend the undeserved mercy that He so graciously bestowed upon me at the moment of my salvation. My heart was softened toward the Lord, and my desires began to turn away from self and toward Jesus.

The ultimate transformation that occurs in the human heart is when we begin to desire the glory of God. That is the essence of becoming a new creation in Christ (2 Cor. 5:17). The old person who was born into sin (love of self) is now new, with a new heart and new desires (Ezek. 36:26–27)—the desire to reflect the radiance of Christ, His light, His goodness, His love, His faithfulness to a dark and hurting world.

Loving Jesus Is the Radiant Christian Life

Precious friends, I so wish I could grab you by the hands and say, "Please don't miss this!" The radiant life is not about a list of rules that we follow or a mold we try to fit. Oh no! Shining as lights in the darkness begins and ends with loving God and His glory. Yes, it is that simple. When we truly love Him, we desire—above all else—to live for His glory.

A few years after I fell in love with Jesus, God gave me an illustration to help me understand this connection more deeply. As we grow in our relationship with God, we begin to see ourselves (the sin we still struggle with) more clearly. As this awareness happened in my life, I was troubled by the presence of sin, yet I mistakenly tried to remedy my problem through human effort: trying harder to be good, and so on. None of these self-efforts worked to change my heart. In my frustration, God brought me back to the primary motivator: love.

As I prayed about the particular sin struggle that I was dealing with, the Lord brought to mind the image of a bride on her wedding day—the very image I described to you at the beginning of this chapter. This vision helped me to see the connection between a bride's desire to look beautiful for her groom and *why* I should hate my own sin and overcome temptation.

Recall the moment when the beautiful, radiant bride is revealed. She stands before her groom and their eyes meet. Can you see her? Gloriously radiant . . .

Now, instead, imagine that her dress is covered in stains, her hair is a hot mess, and her face is smeared with grime. This certainly is not the picture of a radiant bride, is it? Of course not! No girl in the world would willingly show up at her wedding in such a state. Why? Because she loves her groom and wants him to be pleased with her.

Girls, the same proves true for us, the Bride of Christ. The motivation to live pure and holy lives comes from our love for Jesus. We long for the day when we will see His face, and we want to live in a way that pleases Him. The stains of impurity and sin are not befitting a radiant bride; therefore, we avoid and abstain from anything that would bring disgrace to the name of Jesus. We live for His glory!

What's Love Got to Do with It?

Have you ever seen a couple in love and thought to yourself, *I want that!* I recall a friend's wedding. I distinctly remember my reaction when the bride walked down the aisle. There I was wearing my "I promise you'll be able to wear it again" bridesmaid dress, and dreaming about wedding cake, when my friend entered the sanctuary. Of course, she looked beautiful, but when her eyes locked on her groom, her countenance transformed from simply beautiful to radiant in a single glance. As I witnessed her transformation, I heard my heart say, "I want *that*."

I think that is what our love for Jesus is meant to cause in the life of others. When others encounter us, see our love for

Jesus, witness the transforming power of His love in us, they will say, "I want that."

God created us *to reflect His glorious light to the world.* Just as a bride's face reflects the love of her groom, a follower of Jesus reflects Him to the world. The radiance God intends for us is the inner glow of a woman who is redeemed. Forgiven from sin. Loved by God. Filled by His light. She understands that the God of the universe picked her to be His own. She's living the ultimate fairy tale. She knows she's the princess rescued by the prince, chosen and transformed by His love. She is madly in love with Jesus and basks in the glow of His love for her. This relationship is so transforming that the world is able to see it—because she is aglow.

This, my friends, is true radiance.

Unfading.

Unchanging.

Unending.

Radiance for a woman who is in a relationship with Jesus should be a daily reality. Not something that quickly fades when the white dress is packed away or when the honeymoon is over—no, our radiance is meant to last. Radiance is our purpose, our destiny, our calling. Just as the moon reflects the light of the sun, God created us to reflect His light and love to the world.

God is calling forth a generation of radiant women.

Trust me, the darkness around us will only increase day by day. We must choose this day to shine—to love Jesus and let that love spur us on to live for His glory. Remember, we are the light of the world (Matt. 5:14)!

Just as I looked at my friend on her wedding day and longed for the radiance I saw in her, we are created so that when the world looks at us, they see God's love reflected in our face, and say, "I want *that*." Girls, it's time we locked eyes with our heavenly Bridegroom, Jesus Christ, and show the world the radiant glow that results from His love.

SHINE ON!

Recognizing your great need for Jesus
propells us to love Him more.
Allow your sin and brokenness
to lead you to the cross!

"Come here. I'll show you the Bride, the Wife of the Lamb." He took me away in the Spirit to an enormous, high mountain and showed me Holy Jerusalem descending out of Heaven from God, resplendent in the bright glory of God. The City shimmered like a precious gem, light-filled, pulsing light.

Revelation 21:9–11 *The Message*

CHAPTER TWO

A Radiant Woman Reflects
the Radiant One

I've always been fascinated with transformation stories. You know, the ones where the hero or heroine is changed—most of the time for the good. *Beauty and the Beast, Pride and Prejudice, Cinderella, My Fair Lady*—at the heart of each is a tale of transformation.

Take *My Fair Lady* for example. This one is a classic. Definitely a "Girls' Night" flick if you are in the mood for a musical with big hats, luscious costumes, and a barrage of every British dialect you could ever hear short of a ride to Paddington station. My friend and I curled up one rainy morning, coffee in hand, to watch the 1946 musical. The screen flickered alive with colors and motion as we were transported to old London town (so much so that we wanted to trade our beloved hazelnut dark roast for a spot of tea). The music was familiar, having given birth to classics that we hear as background music in malls, sung at talent contests, played by Big Bands at galas, and even piped into elevators.

But the true reason that we were transfixed for almost three hours, pressing the pause button only when absolutely necessary (coffee refills and bathroom breaks), was the play-by-play, step-by-step process of transformation. Our eyes were riveted, our bodies pressed forward toward the screen, staring at the girl who was living out her transformation right before our very eyes.

For those of you who don't know the story, I'll summarize it for you. Eliza Doolittle (played by Audrey Hepburn), a poor street girl with no money, no education, and no dreams, is selling flowers in the town square of Victorian London. Professor Higgins takes her under his wing as a challenge, to "transform her" into a proper lady. He boasted, "You see this creature with her curbstone English, the English that will keep her in the gutter until the end of her days? I say, within six months I could pass her off as a duchess at the Embassy Ball."

The wager was made. He would transform her from a poor street girl to a duchess. At this time in history the class ranks were impenetrable, and dialect was an enormous factor in keeping the classes separate. His goal was not one of kindness and altruism but the opposite, in fact. His goal was to take the ultimate challenge, to take a nobody and trick high society with her grace, charm, and articulation.

My favorite scene is the moment when Eliza departs Professor Higgins's home for the ball dressed like a queen. Her makeover is complete. The former shop girl, who only months before entered that house covered in grime and without poise or confidence, now leaves a new woman. Her transformation is not just one of dress and dialect. She sees herself differently, and Eliza gracefully walks out the door as a lady. She now walks like a lady, dresses like a lady, and talks like a lady. She has spent time absorbing the attributes of the image she wants to reflect. And because she is truly reflecting an inner change, she is radiant with an authenticity that has produced not merely an imitator but a transformed woman.

Eliza Doolittle's tale of transformation strikes a chord in the human heart, as most great stories of its kind do. Admit it, we all love the moments when Cinderella goes to the ball, when the losing baseball team wins the pennant, when the ugly duckling becomes a swan, or in this case when poor Eliza becomes a duchess. The chord is tuned to the eternal song of redemption, and this redemption is found to be more powerful than the physical transformation or validation we often long for on earth.

The word *redemption* means to "buy something back and to restore it to its original intent." Every human heart beats to be redeemed, restored to our original intention. Instinctively, we know that we were created for more. We were indeed created for glory, formed to manifest radiance. Christianity is the ultimate transformation story. You and I are invited into a relationship with God, and in this relationship we are transformed from the inside out—from darkness to light. Jesus takes our brokenness and forms something beautiful. We are transformed into a masterpiece for which only He could get the glory. Miraculously, sinners become saints, the lost are found, and the blind can see.

Originally the term *Christian* was coined to describe a group of people whose lives displayed the teachings and characteristics of Jesus Christ. His life was evident in them, and as a result, they were slanderously labeled Christ-ians. Oh how I wish that would be said of us today! Too often we claim His name without representing His heart. Today the term Christian is given because we attend church or grow up in a certain culture, and not because we are people who live like Jesus. Radiance is the call to live out our faith, evidence to a watching world of our relationship with our Redeemer.

How does this great work occur? This transformation begins the moment our eyes are opened to see Jesus and continues as we follow Him, becoming conformed more to His likeness. And we are not on our own. Like Eliza Doolittle we have a tutor, though He is infinitely more compassionate, holy, and perfect. The Holy Spirit is our guide to and through our transformation process. The Spirit nudges and directs us to reflect what is pure, what is true, and what is radiant, for the glory of our Redeemer. As the apostle Paul writes, "We all, with unveiled faces, are looking as in a mirror at the glory of the Lord and are being transformed into the same image from glory to glory" (2 Cor. 3:18 HCSB).

This all sounds good, doesn't it? But how do we really live this out on a daily basis? How is this supposed to change our behavior on campus, during a Pilates class, or in line at Starbucks? How do we show a world that desperately needs to see authentic transformation that faith in Christ really works? In a world of fake purses, virtual communication, and absurd reality TV, people long for the genuine article. Very few people will believe our message if they don't see it lived out daily in our lives. It is one thing to say that a Christian is "light in the darkness," but to actually live that is putting your money where your mouth is. And girls, our calling is to live our faith so authentically that others are drawn to our Savior.

In their book *Shine*, Christian recording artists the Newsboys discuss the power and importance of our light in this world:

> There is no better way to make a meaningful impact on the world than by becoming God's children of light—by living lives that are so free of obstructions that His light is unhindered. People today don't accept what they hear at face value. They want to know that it works. They want to see that it works. If not, they will move on to something else. They're not different from us. They have problems, needs, questions, and hopes. But they won't necessarily recognize that these things can be only answered in Christ without seeing that fact demonstrated— in us. We are the hope of the world, because as

we reflect Christ's life, we enable them to see Him clearly.[1]

How will the world see Jesus in us? Allow me to get more personal: How will the world see Jesus in *you*? Take a moment to silently answer. That's a hard one, isn't it? Here is what you need to know. The type of radical transformation that this quote describes begins and ends with revelation. The word *revelation* means to reveal, to disclose, to make known. When we see Jesus, truly behold Him and know Him, He transforms us. It is this revelation that produces transformation.

Revelation Produces Transformation

Take Moses for example. He is a great place for us to start because he actually had a face-to-face mountaintop encounter with God, Himself. In fact, this is where we get the phrase "mountaintop experience." But it all began much earlier. Moses' transformation actually began with a burning bush. The glorious sight captivated his attention. This mysterious fire drew him aside to explore how it could be that it was on fire yet not consumed. Moses inched closer, and from the midst of the burning bush, the Angel of the Lord spoke, breaking four hundred years of silence between God and His people.

For Moses, this was no ordinary day. After forty years of living in insignificance, tending sheep for his father-in-law, Moses' life was about to change dramatically. In fact all of history hinged on this moment; God would send forth Moses as the deliverer to redeem His people from the bondage of slavery—beautifully foreshadowing the sending of His own Son to deliver humanity from darkness to light. Once he could breathe normally again, that moment changed everything for Moses. The God of the universe had revealed Himself, and this disclosure changed the course of his life, setting his feet on a path of glory. Little did Moses know where this path of glory would take him; first, to Egypt where glory was displayed but then, most importantly, up a mountain where glory was beheld.

After seeing glimpses of the Holy One, the *Great I Am*, display His might and power along the journey from Egypt to the Promised Land, Moses understood there was more to this God than could be grasped with the human mind. Incomprehensible yet, still, he wanted to know Him more. He was not satisfied with seeing the work of His hands; He longed to see His face . . . to know Him.

This man was not the one we might expect to be found on the mountaintop, so to speak. He narrowly escaped genocide at birth by being abandoned, was adopted by those enslaving God's people, and eventually committed murder. This is not the résumé we would expect for one who desires to know God. Yet, "Show me Your glory!!" was his bold prayer. And the God who first spoke to him from the bush—who defeated Pharaoh, who led His people with a fire by night and a cloud by day, who brought water from a rock and bread from heaven—was pleased with Moses' desire. He directed Moses back up the mountain, told him exactly where to stand, and gave him a glimpse of His glory. I try to put myself in Moses' sandals as he made the trek from the Israelite camp to the top of Mount Sinai to meet with God. Clearly, Moses did not take this privilege lightly. After all, he'd witnessed the wrath of the Lord toward His enemies, and the incredible fact that God favored and loved them was inconceivable, yet Moses knew, "God does love us."

What I see in Moses is desire. More than wanting provision from the Lord, Moses wanted to experience His presence. Nothing in the world could compete with simply being *with* Him. It was this longing that overcame his fear of the Lord's holiness and kept him moving up the mountain, pressing into the cloud, to wait for God. There, at the top of the mountain, the Lord God Almighty descended, and His glory passed by Moses as he hid in the cleft of a rock.

Revelation

What is God's glory? It is the splendor of His person, His character, His name, and His majesty. It is the revelation of the person of God. To give Moses a glimpse, God spoke, revealing His glorious character: *"The LORD, the LORD, the compassionate and gracious God, slow to anger, abounding in love and faithfulness, maintaining love to thousands, and forgiving wickedness, rebellion, and sin. Yet he does not leave the guilty unpunished; he punishes the children and their children for the sin of the fathers to the third and fourth generation"* (Exod. 34:6–7).

At this revelation Moses bowed down and worshipped.

Afraid to budge, his soul found for the first time the very reason for its existence: glory. Moses lingered in God's presence—forty days and forty nights to be precise. Wave after wave of love, like an ocean of goodness, engulfed him in the presence of His Majesty. Nothing in our natural world can compare . . . his soul was overwhelmed by the fire, but like the infamous bush, miraculously he was not destroyed.

Beholding.

Worshipping.

Adoring.

Listening.

I'm sure Moses would still be there today had the Lord not sent him back down the mountain to lead the people.

Transformation

Moses did not realize that the revelation of God's glory had transformed him. Of course, he knew he'd never be the same again after experiencing God, but Moses had no idea that transformation was evident to all; he was unaware of his own radiance.

> When Moses came down from Mount Sinai with the two tablets of the Testimony in his hands, he was not aware that **his face was radiant** because he had spoken with the LORD. When Aaron and all the Israelites saw Moses, **his face was radiant,** and they were afraid to come near him. But Moses called

to them; so Aaron and all the leaders of the community came back to him, and he spoke to them. Afterward all the Israelites came near him, and he gave them all the commands the LORD had given him on Mount Sinai. When Moses finished speaking to them, he put a veil over his face. But whenever he entered **the LORD's presence** to speak with him, he removed the veil until he came out. And when he came out and told the Israelites what had been commanded, they **saw that his face was radiant**. (Exod. 34:29–35, emphasis added)

When Moses came down from meeting with the Lord his face glowed—evidence of time spent in the presence of God.

Reflecting the Radiant One

God has called each of His children to radiance, to reflect His glory to the world. Like Moses, we do this by beholding Him. How does this happen? When we look to Jesus, who is the fullness of God's glory, we, too, are transformed. The Bible says, *"The Son is the **radiance of God's glory** and the exact representation of his being, sustaining all things by his powerful word"* (Heb. 1:3, emphasis added). Jesus is the Radiant One who reveals to us the glory of God. When we turn to Him in faith, beholding the glory of the Lord, like Moses, we are transformed. Our radiance is simply a reflection of Jesus, the Radiant One.

For God, who said, "Let light shine out of darkness," made **his light** shine in our hearts to give us **the light of the knowledge of the glory of God in the face of Christ**. (2 Cor. 4:6, emphasis added)

In the beginning was the Word [Jesus Christ],
and the Word was with God,
and the Word was God. . . . The Word became
    flesh
and took up residence among us.
We observed His glory,
the glory as the One and Only Son from the
    Father,
full of grace and truth. (John 1:1, 14)

But whenever anyone turns to the Lord, the veil is taken away. Now the Lord is the Spirit, and where the Spirit of the Lord is, there is freedom. And we, who with unveiled faces all **reflect the Lord's glory**, are being **transformed into his likeness** with ever-increasing glory, which comes from the Lord, who is the Spirit. (2 Cor. 3:16–18 NIV, emphasis added)

These Scriptures pretty much sum up my life experience. To say that I've been transformed is the understatement of all understatements. We are talking extreme makeover! Yet, I was not changed by following a set of rules or listening to one of those cheesy self-help motivational speakers, nor was I under the instruction from a great tutor like Eliza Doolittle. No, my life changed—completely, radically, totally transformed—from time spent beholding Jesus, the Radiant One.

Here's the deal, salvation is just the beginning of our relationship with Jesus. It is only the first step on the road toward radiance. Many people claim faith in Jesus, yet their lives don't show evidence of transformation. The reason? Radiance requires exposure to His presence. Real and lasting transformation occurs when we spend time with Him, beholding His glory and in turn reflecting His character.

We are to make Jesus visible to the world—His love, grace, truth, kindness, humility, gentleness, patience, generosity, and compassion. When His life shines through ours, then the darkness around us is illuminated. In the midst of a world that asks, "What's in it for me?" a Christian's genuine love for others and selfless compassion spotlights the transforming work of God in our hearts. It is this type of life change that causes the world to sit up and take notice of our faith.

How does this happen? This kind of transformation occurred in my life when I began to prioritize spending time with Jesus and seeking Him through the reading of His Word. Supernaturally my life began to change. When I fell in love with Jesus, I desired to spend time with Him. We meet with God through the reading of His Word and prayer. In these times of devotion, our hearts are exposed to His glorious presence. Like Moses whose face reflected the glory of God, the result of our meeting with Jesus is that we, too, reflect His glorious character to the world: "For you were once darkness, but now you are light in the Lord. Live as children of light" (Eph. 5:8).

Son-Kissed Glow

I burn easily. As a blonde, blue-eyed, pale-skinned girl, it happens. My first few summer outings always produce a nice red burn on my skin, the visible evidence of my time in the sun. Although I love the look of a sun-kissed glow, I realize it is not great for my skin or my health. During a recent weekend getaway to the beach, I was reminded that my fair skin needs sunscreen.

Dining outside for lunch on a beautiful pier that overlooked the San Diego bay, I lazily enjoyed my Cobb salad as my winter-weary skin soaked up a few rays. This weekend was one of those much-needed breaks when I could get lost in a good book and simply enjoy the view as the kind waiter refilled my iced tea for hours. Of course I totally forgot sunscreen. Who remembers such things when engrossed in Jane Austen? I don't.

Sure enough, when I returned to my hotel room, I saw the evidence of my afternoon in the sun: the glaring white line against pink flesh proved I'd been overexposed. Every dermatologist in the world would caution me against overexposure to the sun. Yet, as I was scolding myself for forgetting something so important, I thought, *Thankfully, there is one exposure that we can't ever get too much of, and that is exposure to* the Son, *Jesus Christ, who is the Light of the World.*

The more we see Jesus, behold Him, and worship Him . . . we are transformed. Like Moses, our lives reflect the Radiant One. Just as time in the sun is evidenced on our skin, so time with the Son is evidenced in our lives.

The next morning in San Diego, I woke up and spent time reading God's Word and talking to Him. Later that afternoon I went for a run down the Pacific coastline. With worship music blaring through my iPod, my heart was full of praises for my God as I beheld the beauty of His creation and pondered His incredible goodness. Exposed to the power and presence of the King of kings and Lord of lords, I was humbled that this great and mighty God knows me by name and rescued me from darkness to live as the light of the world.

Walking back to my car while still worshipping the Son, I spotted a woman smoking her cigarette and mumbling on the street corner. From a distance she blended in with the bustling activity. The people hurrying past kept their eyes fixed, up and away from her, toward their destination. After all, it's easier not to feel when you just don't look. Who really wants to think about people like this while in the lap of luxury? It would have been so easy not to see her. But that's the thing about exposure to the Son, you start to see things—people, places, and situations—as He sees them.

I was propelled from within to go to her. I walked over, knelt down, gave her my emergency fund from my running shorts pouch, and spent some time getting to know Nancy. I listened to her story; the chain of unfortunate events that led her to be homeless. She told me about the bed she kept across the street in the alley and the kind people at the church who helped her out when she got in a bind. We talked about Jesus, and then, together, we talked to Jesus.

Walking away I was struck by the experience. How completely natural and normal it felt. Not contrived, planned, or pressured. I didn't sign up to minister to the homeless, nor did I premeditate giving to someone in need. I simply responded and reacted to life as a result of spending time with Jesus . . . His love overflowing my heart.

No one had to tell me to give.

No one had to tell me to care.

No one had to tell me to pray.

Honestly, I didn't care one bit if people saw me talking to her. To tell you the truth, I didn't think about people at all until I stood up and realized that a group of ten or so was standing behind me, staring.

Please know that I don't tell you this story to puff myself up or to seem "super spiritual" in your eyes (because trust me, I'm not!). Too many times I've failed to reflect Jesus to the world. I share this story because I learned a powerful truth that day about radiance. Reflecting the love and light of Christ to a broken world is the natural response when we spend time worshipping Him. The more time we spend in the presence of Jesus, the Light of the World, the more others will see that Son-kissed glow on us.

Friends, as you and I encounter Christ on a daily basis, through reading His Word and through prayer, we are changed.

Jesus gives us His eyes to see, His heart to feel, His words to speak, and His thoughts to think. As we are conformed to be more like Him, we become radiant women who are lit from within by His love.

SHINE ON!

Want to experience true transformation? Establish time with Jesus as the top priority of your day.

If anyone is in Christ, he is a new creation;
the old has gone, the new has come!

2 Corinthians 5:17

CHAPTER THREE

A Radiant Woman Remembers
Her True Identity

The phrase "I pulled a Marian" means only one thing in my circle of friends. Someone, usually yours truly, has forgotten something. I like to think my forgetfulness is endearing, although I'm sure if you were to poll my closest buddies, they'd probably say they find it quite annoying at times. Thankfully, I have sweet friends who extend much grace. I forget things ALL THE TIME! My keys, my phone, my purse, my medicine, my gym key, my speaking notes. I'm used to living with myself by now . . . we've been together a really long time. I've grown in self-acceptance, and I'm extremely fond of sticky notes.

Flashback . . .

To celebrate high school graduation, my girlfriends and I went on a Caribbean cruise. Look out Jamaica, Grand Cayman, and Cozumel—ten Texas girls coming your way! This was my first excursion out of the country, and I'd planned and day-dreamed about this trip for months. I dieted (months on Slim Fast is not a fond memory); I packed for weeks prior to our departure and worked hard to pay for the trip.

The morning of the cruise, we drove five hours from my small hometown to our destination in New Orleans where the ship was docked. With images dancing through my head of the exotic locations that awaited me, I gleefully schlepped my lug-gage up to the boarding dock. While singing the theme song to "The Love Boat," my turn to check in arrived and my blissful moment came to a crushing halt when I realized, "OH NO!!! I PULLED A MARIAN!"

In my excitement I forgot the one thing I really needed. No, not my swimsuit; I packed nine of those. Yes, I remembered sunscreen, spending money, a sundry of sundresses, and enough mindless reading to last as long as Gilligan's cruise. Of course, I left the one thing that mattered most, my identification. You know, a passport, a driver's license, or even a birth certificate. I was sans any form of legit ID.

For those of you new to international travel, as I was at that age, a girl can't just hop out of the country with a wink and a smile. Trust me, I tried it. Oh no, that pesky ship captain and his crew were oh so picky about proof of citizenship and such.

Never fear friends, they were *not* leaving me behind!

I was determined to get my Slim-Fast-self on that boat; months on a liquid diet had left me cranky and unwavering in my mission. Over my dead malnourished body would they leave me in New Orleans!

Thanks to Momma Jordan faxing my birth certificate, my best friend's prom picture displaying the two of us with our school's name, and a whole lot of persuasion by yours truly, I convinced Captain Stubing to let me aboard. Aloha!

Identity in Christ

Forgetting one's ID is a huge problem when it comes to international travel, yet globe-trotting is not the only situation in which forgetting an identification is problematic. When it comes to living out our Christian faith and heeding the call to be "light in the darkness," we must be women who remember our identity in Christ.

Some of you may be saying, wait a minute, the last time I checked my purse, I had a driver's license, social security card, movie rental card, and a pass to my local library. I have no idea what you mean by "identity in Christ." Since this is one of those Christian phrases that is often thrown around, but rarely explained, let's examine the meaning. Let me break it down for you.

Just as identification cards answer the question, "Who am I?," *our* God-given identity in Christ answers the same question. For example, my passport clearly identifies me as a citizen of the

United States of America. Likewise, God's Word clearly identifies me as a citizen of the kingdom of God. With this new citizenship, the Bible declares that I have a new name, a new status, and a new purpose. As 2 Corinthians 5:17 states, "if anyone is in Christ, he is a *new creation*; the old is gone, the new has come!" As new creations in Christ, we are no longer identified as we were before; now, our identity is based upon and shaped by who God says we are as His children. Why is that important? The reason is simple: we "behave how we believe." *Our actions and attitudes stem from our self-perception. So many people attempt to change their actions by sheer will or through discipline, not understanding that most of what we do is based upon our identity; therefore, we must start at the beginning.*

A Lesson from a Pig

> We cannot consistently behave in ways that are different from what we believe about ourselves.
>
> —Kenneth Boa

When I was a little girl, my family lived on a small farm in Texas. I did not appreciate the blessing of the simple life back then as I do now. Yet, I do have unforgettable memories of the games we played and the trouble we got into living on a farm loaded with a barn, fishing pond, vegetable garden, and miles of country roads. Adventures awaited me each day with chickens, horses, cows, and some of the meanest ducks west of the

Mississippi. Some of my greatest life lessons were learned on that farm. The biggest one is this: **We behave how we believe**.

In addition to the horses and chickens, we also owned and fed a bunch of dogs. Little ones and big ones, all mutts of various breeds, and most only good for chasing the occasional car that would drive down the farm road. In the midst of that pack of Purina-pounding, good-for-nothing, car-chasing canines stood a lone pig. As in swine, pork, bacon . . . you know, like Miss Piggy (without the attitude, of course).

This was no ordinary pig. This pig had a huge identity crisis. Living amidst a pack of dogs, our pig would chase cars, eat dog food, and make the funniest little dog-like bark you've ever heard. Why? It *believed* it was a dog. It did not remember that it was a pig. All it saw all day long, hour after hour, was dog behavior; therefore, it believed that was how a pig was supposed to behave.

You get it? We behave how we believe.

The same problem faces Christian women today. We live in a world filled with selfishness, pride, lust, rage, materialism, and greed that bombards us with images and messages designed to shape and mold our identity and, consequently, our behavior into its image. Although God called us out of the darkness to live as lights in the world, like my pig, because we see these images all day long, we think certain behaviors and attitudes are normal. Yet these are not "normal" for Christians because we are no longer citizens of this world.

Our enemy is not stupid. He knows that if he can win the battle for our minds, and thereby influence and determine our identity, he has our lives. Although he can never take our salvation, he can sure destroy our testimonies.

Don't Conform . . . Be Transformed

Friends, I have a question for you. Does your lifestyle reflect the glory of God, or like my pig, are you modeling your behavior and attitudes to fit the company you keep or the images you see in the media? Are you living out your identity as a child of God who He has called "the light of the world"? Or are you conforming to the lifestyle of people who don't know Jesus? I know all too well how easy it is to get sucked into the world's lifestyle. Yet, the following passage is clear . . . we can't conform to this world; the Word of God must transform us. Our identities must be shaped by who He says we are: *"Don't copy the behavior and customs of this world, but let God transform you into a new person by changing the way you think. Then you will learn to know God's will for you, which is good and pleasing and perfect"* (Rom. 12:2 NLT).

Before I met Jesus, my identity was formed primarily by my culture and my experiences. My culture shaped me in many ways (through movies, television, and education) into its mold. From this mold emerged a woman who lived for people's approval, feared rejection, hated her body, lived a dangerous and promiscuous lifestyle, and believed her worth was found in gaining a guy's attention. My culture convinced me that my ID read "usable object."

Is it any wonder that sexual sin is such a huge issue among Christians? We've allowed the enemy to identify us as something we are not: sexual objects. Therefore, one of the driving forces of *Redeemed Girl Ministries* is to transform the thinking of women to know and believe their worth and live out their true identity in Christ. I'll say it again—we behave how we believe. If we see ourselves as usable, we will allow others to treat us as such, but if we see ourselves as priceless treasures, we will act like them. And in turn, we will expect others to treat us as treasures. This concept is so vital for young women today. The enemy's lie not only degrades us but leaves us feeling used and worthless. God alone is able to declare any woman's true worth, for He is God. God desires for us to know we are worth so much more; we are a treasure worth dying for!

It's Time for a New Identity

As radiant women, we embrace our identity in Christ. We do so, first and foremost, by understanding it. In 1 Peter 2:9–12, we find several key truths that, if believed, will transform a woman's life.

> But you are a chosen people, a royal priesthood, a
> holy nation, a people belonging to God, that you
> may declare the praises of him who called you out

of darkness into his wonderful light. Once you were not a people, but now you are the people of God; once you had not received mercy, but now you have received mercy. Dear friends, I urge you, as aliens and strangers in the world, to abstain from sinful desires, which war against your soul. Live such good lives among the pagans that, though they accuse you of doing wrong, they may see your good deeds and glorify God on the day he visits us.

From this passage, we will examine the following three phrases that are essential for every radiant woman to believe about her identity:

1. I am chosen and loved by God.
2. I am a member of the royal priesthood.
3. I am holy.

I Am Chosen and Loved by God

Every girl wants to be picked. It's a girl thing, I guess. I am convinced that the only reason the television show *The Bachelor* has a leg to stand on is because the producers know that they can manipulate this desire in women. Every season, smart and beautiful girls clamor to hear one question: "Will you accept this rose?" With the offer of the blessed bud comes the coveted truth that she is singled out and chosen. Oh, the sheer joy that sweeps across a face when those words are spoken.

Being chosen makes a girl feel loved.

If we're being honest, we recognize that deep within the heart of every woman is a profound need to feel loved. Married or single, young or old, this need drives us; therefore, we look out to the world and ask, "What do I need to do or to be in order to be lovable?" Like a soldier reporting for duty, we stand by, awaiting orders and jumping at the world's commands. The world sends us the message loud and clear, "You are un-lovable unless you are . . ."

- pretty enough
- thin enough
- smart enough
- rich enough
- popular enough

Throughout our lives we hear these messages. We allow them to sink into our psyches, and, like my pet pig of yonder years, we adapt our lives and behaviors to do whatever we think it will take to make us lovable. The result is a sad one. An endless and exhausting cycle of futility awaits all of us who attempt to *earn* love.

As I've grown older, I've experienced this battle in almost every arena. The temptation to find my identity in something other than Jesus (my weight, my income, my boyfriend—or lack thereof—my looks, etc.). The battle is always present. I must choose to find my worth and value in Him. The reality is . . .

We are never pretty enough.

We are never thin enough.

We are never smart enough.

We are never rich enough.

You get the idea. The ache for love is never satisfied . . . the nagging question still remains: is this good enough to earn love? For this reason, the first thing we, as followers of Jesus are told is this: **You are chosen and loved by God**. This is not something you can earn. This is **who you are**.

When the Bible teaches us to "be transformed by the renewing of our minds," understanding that we are loved is the first place most of us need to start. We've been programmed, or brainwashed even, to think that we must perform or strive in order to earn love. Yet, God says that is not how it works. We can't earn love; we *are* loved. The following verses from Ephesians explain this life-changing truth.

> All praise to God, the Father of our Lord Jesus Christ, who has blessed us with every spiritual blessing in the heavenly realms because we are united with Christ. **Even before he made the world, God loved us and chose us in Christ to be holy and without fault in his eyes. God decided in advance to adopt us into his own family by bringing us to himself through Jesus Christ.** This is what he wanted to do, and it gave him great pleasure. (Eph. 1:3–5 NLT, emphasis added)

First of all, when did God choose us? "Before he made the world." Stop. Imagine. Ponder this truth with me. Before

God spoke the universe into orbit, before He said, "Let there be . . . ," He saw us. He loved us. He chose us. He picked us. Not only that, but I love that the Bible also tells us that it gave God "great pleasure" to choose us and bestow His love upon us.

What gives you great pleasure? A vacation . . . alone time . . . date night . . . chocolate ice cream . . . watching a sunset? Please don't miss this. God took "great pleasure" in choosing *you*. Think about it this way, He was more excited to offer you the rose than you were to hear your name called.

He loves to love you.

Believing this truth grants you a precious gift, the blessing of a settled identity. Instead of a life filled with chronic insecurity and striving or constant conforming and transforming into the latest measure of perfection, you who believe God's Word can know in the deepest places of your heart that you are loved. Nothing and no one can change that fact.

Our identity in Christ says to us that we, at the core of our being, are loved. Wherever you are right now, I want you to stop reading and say to yourself, "I am chosen and loved by God." I pray you will own this truth. I pray you will ponder and meditate on these verses and allow God to penetrate the places in your heart where you live in fear. Just as there are consequences for forgetting a passport, there are huge consequences when you forget that you are loved. Your life is one marred by fear.

Fear of failure.

Fear of rejection.

Fear of not being "good" enough.

To fear is to live in dread, angst, or worry. All sorts of fears plague a life that is not at rest in God's love. The Word of God tells us, "Perfect love casts out fear" (1 John 4:18 NASB). Perfect love is God's love. It is described as perfect because it is unchanging, unwavering, unshakable, and unstoppable. We can't un-earn it, and we can't lose it. Taking hold of our God-given identity can free us from all sorts of self-worth related issues that are rooted in fear: eating disorders, sexual sin, cutting, perfectionism, and addictions. At the heart of these issues, lies a fear that we won't be loved or accepted unless we meet some standard.

In Christ, we don't need to follow the world's way of working for love and striving after acceptance and worth because the issue is settled. God proved His love for us in the sacrificial death of His Son, Jesus, on the cross. *God demonstrates his own love for us in this: While we were still sinners, Christ died for us"* (Rom. 5:8).

Therefore, we don't need to fear not being perfect, not meeting the world's standards, not maintaining an image in order to earn love. God's perfect love says we are chosen and loved exactly the way we are. . . . Settled. Finished. Done.

Let's be honest, most of us know God loves us, but I realize that truly believing and receiving His love on a personal level can be difficult. Recently I watched a movie that helped me comprehend the depth of God's love for us, and the extent to which He went to demonstrate His love.

The movie *Taken* is about a wealthy teenage girl from a divorced home. Her biological father, played by Liam Neeson, desires a relationship with her so he moves to her city in order to pursue his goal. Neeson is a retired government operative who is highly skilled in intelligence. His background and training cause him to seem rigidly overprotective when his daughter, who is only seventeen, seeks his permission to spend the summer in Paris with a friend.

Aware of the dangers that the girls could encounter, the father says no; but later he changes his mind and allows the trip. She pledges to follow his rules and abide by his terms. Yet, upon her arrival in Paris, he learns that he didn't really know the full story about her and her friend's plans for the visit. But it is too late. Members of an Albanian crime ring kidnap the two girls and smuggle them into the underground sex trafficking movement in France.

A father's worst nightmare has occurred. His daughter is missing; she is in the hands of monsters whose intentions are evil. He must act—and quickly. He is a man on a mission: to save his daughter.

As I watched this film, I sat on the edge of my seat, breathless. My whole body was involved in the action. I felt my pulse quicken as the father vowed his intention to rescue her from the wicked men. My stomach knotted as I realized she was sold into a sex trafficking ring and her future was slavery. But her father did not give up. We cheered as her father systematically tracked down the villains, knocking down doors to reach his daughter locked inside. I nearly stood up and clapped at the end of the movie when the man holding Neeson's daughter yelled to the other villain, "It's the girls' father and he wants her back."

You want to know why I loved this movie? *Taken* gives us glimpses of God's love for us. Granted, these glimpses are in the form of a script and Hollywood action scenes, but from it I was reminded of the intense passion of God to redeem and rescue His children from the grip of sin and death. It reminds us of the heart of God that says, "You are worth fighting for."

Like the daughter in this film, we, too, rebelled. And likewise, we are held captive to an enemy whose intention is to kill, to steal, and to destroy (John 10:10). *But God!* He didn't leave us in our mess. He didn't abandon us even though we've rebelled. No! The Bible tells us in Romans 5:8 that "while we were still sinners, Christ died for us." He didn't just leave us to suffer and to deal with the consequences of our rebellion. He kicked the door of sin down with the cross, and with His outstretched arms He said, "I want you back!"

My purpose in sharing this with you is, I know how hard it can be at times to believe, truly believe, that God loves *you*. Our feelings can be similar to those of the daughter in *Taken*, who is shocked when her dad crashes through the door to rescue her and looks at him in disbelief and asks, "You came for me?" She absolutely couldn't believe her father's love would fight her enemy in order to rescue her.

Take this truth to heart. Jesus came to Earth to fight for you! The God of the universe died to deliver you and me from slavery. Yes, *you*. He wants you to know and believe that you are worth dying for. When you choose to believe this truth, everything changes.

So many women struggle with an identity that is not based in God's love. I totally get this one. I wore labels of all sorts before Jesus, in His love, said to me, "You aren't that girl anymore." Believing my true identity transformed me from the inside out. A woman whose identity is settled in the love of God is free. Free from striving. Free from insecurity. Free from the prison of perfectionism.

If we are going to be radiant women who reflect the light of Christ to the world, then we must believe that we are loved. If not, we will fall for the deceptive lies of the world that desires to pull us back into its prisons of fear, shame, and insecurity. When we believe the lies of the world that say we are nothing more than sexual objects, or that our worth is found in meeting some elusive measure of perfection, we see ourselves as usable and unlovable. We don't believe that we have intrinsic worth and that we are far more valuable than our boob size. (Yes, I just went there.)

No more! Radiant woman . . . say with me, "I am loved!"

When we begin to believe we are loved, the light that shines from our lives will be brilliant!

I Am a Member of the Royal Priesthood

When you and I placed our faith in Christ, we became citizens of the kingdom of God (Col. 1:13). As we've said before, with this new citizenship comes a new identity. In addition to the fact that we are "loved and chosen," 1 Peter 2:9 also tells us that we are now members of a "royal priesthood."

Before you freak out and think this means a life of drab clothing with a white collar, please chill. To be a member of the royal priesthood of God is not about a vocation or wardrobe; it is a title that means we are of the privileged ones who have access into His very presence. No longer are we excluded because of sin; we have a "back stage pass," so to speak, into the very throne room of God.

In the Old Testament, the priests serving in God's temple offered sacrifices and prayers on behalf of the people. Members of the priesthood were the only ones who could enter into the holiest place in the temple and meet with God personally. Now that privilege is bestowed upon all of God's children because of our faith in Jesus. We don't need anyone to go to God for us; we have the right and freedom to go ourselves.

Why does the title Royal Priesthood matter? Knowing this identity with its privileged access to God, greatly influences our role as radiant women. Remember Moses? His face was radiant from the time spent in the presence of God. The same is true for us. We must spend time with Jesus, and when we behold Him—the Light of the World—we experience the transformation that occurs simply by being with Him. Yet, if we do not intentionally enter God's presence in worship and prayer, then we don't experience that transformation.

Here's the deal. Satan knows how this works. He knows full well that when you and I spend time with God our character becomes like His, thereby reflecting His glorious light to the world. Therefore, Satan does not want us to "enter in" and take advantage of our position as members of the royal priesthood. Think about it:

- Have you ever tried to pray and felt bombarded by thoughts of how unworthy you are?
- Have you ever tried to read your Bible and felt like God was angry with you?
- Have you ever tried to worship and felt like you couldn't praise God for some reason?

The enemy loves to play mind tricks on us to keep us from spending time with God. He fears our radiance. So, he tries to convince us that we are unworthy, unclean, or unacceptable to God. Our enemy would love for us to forget our identity as members of the royal priesthood—to forget that we have the privilege of entering the very throne room of God.

Not only have I forgotten my passport before an international trip, but also I've forgotten my identity as a member of the royal priesthood. On days when I've "blown it big time," I've felt like God would reject me and wouldn't allow me to come to Him because of my sin. Believing this lie delayed my running to the cross and asking for the forgiveness that is mine because of Christ. I fell for the schemes of the devil who wanted me to run away from God instead of *to God*.

Satan is a liar! Jesus tells us this fact in John 8:44. If we are children of God, we always have access into His presence. That access was earned for us by Jesus' death on the cross. The way was cleared for us and we are always welcomed. Check out this powerful truth from Hebrews 10:19–22:

> Therefore, brothers, since we have confidence to enter the Most Holy Place by the blood of Jesus, by a new and living way opened for us through the curtain, that is, his body, and since we have a great high priest over the house of God, let us draw near to God with a sincere heart in full assurance of faith, having our hearts sprinkled to cleanse us from a guilty conscious and having our bodies washed with pure water.

Grab hold tightly to this life-changing truth. If you are a child of God because of Jesus Christ, then you have full access to Him. Nothing can take away your right to enter. Jesus paid the price with His death on the cross. Can't you see how this fact can cause a girl to glow? When you are free from fear and know that you are loved, it will show on your face.

Radiance is a result of a relationship with Jesus. Friends, let us believe God. Let us believe Him when He says that we are members of the royal priesthood. Run boldly to Him; we are always welcome in His presence.

I Am Holy

I have this strange hobby. I collect antique teacups. I know, I know, it sounds quite old-lady-like, but I prefer to think that it brings out the Jane Austen in me. Not sure if my collection is more Sense or Sensibility? But, I digress . . .

Typically, I acquire a new teacup while traveling to different cities. Currently I have cups from London, Prague, Charleston, Vienna, New York, Budapest, Sydney, as well as dozens of small towns and byways in between. My collection serves as a reminder of the various places I've visited and ministered over the years. It's quite lovely.

On a recent trip to South Carolina, I told my friend that I'd love to stop by a local antique store and purchase a cup in honor of her city. She kindly obliged and directed us to a wonderful china shop.

I should have known I was in big trouble the minute I had to ring a buzzer just to get through the locked door. Normally I shop at flea markets and thrift stores, and my teacups average about fifteen dollars. Oh no, not this place. Here, two posh French poodles greeted me the minute my feet hit the exquisite carpeted floors. Unaware of my predicament, within a few minutes I eyed a beautiful cup in a china pattern I didn't own. I asked the saleslady to take it off the shelf so I could inspect it closer. Divine! Like the Little Mermaid with her treasures, I gladly told the kind southern lady, "I'll take it!"

Fumbling through my purse to grab my fifteen dollars to pay, I gasped when the saleslady said, "That will be $253." The room began to spin, and a cold sweat immediately poured down my back. Fumbling to make sense of the mistake, my pride was mortified and kicking into high gear because it knew that I must tell this kind woman there was a big problem. I could not afford, nor could I ever dream to justify, paying more for a teacup than I did for my plane ticket.

As I was forming the words to end the sale and confess my embarrassment, my sweet friend reached out and handed the saleslady her credit card. She wanted to pay for the teacup. Of course a battle ensued. I could not allow her to pay for such an expensive treasure. She insisted and said that it was my graduation gift from seminary. After a few more minutes of arguing, I finally caved (it is quite pretty, after all).

I have a question for you. How do you think I treat that teacup, knowing, as I do, how valuable it is? Do you think I toss it around like a used Starbucks cup? No, of course not. I treat the cup based on its value. I treat it like a precious treasure. I treat it based upon its worth. This teacup is set apart from the rest in my collection. I know the price that was paid for it, and I make sure it is protected and treasured.

When God calls you and me "holy," what He is telling us is that we are set apart; we are not common. For something or someone to be considered "holy" in the Bible, that person or thing was "set apart" to God for Himself and treated in a special manner because of that distinction. The Bible reminds us that understanding our identity transforms our behavior when it says, "Do not conform to the evil desires you had when you lived in ignorance. But just as he who called you is holy, so be holy in all you do" (1 Pet. 1:14–15). We are holy because we are His.

I realize that many readers may squirm at the title "holy." In our culture, the word has a ring of rigid self-righteousness to it. Please erase that image from your thinking. Holiness is simply a reflection of our value and our position as a child of God. The Bible tells us that you and I were not purchased with silver or gold from our empty way of life, but with the precious blood of Christ (1 Pet. 1:18–19). God paid the highest price possible to call us His own—the death of His only Son. Consequently, we are His—and He is holy. *"You are a people holy to the LORD your God. The LORD your God has chosen you out of all the peoples on the face of the earth to be his people, his treasured possession"* (Deut. 7:6).

Like my expensive teacup, God sees you and me as His treasure. That's what holiness is about. Living a life that reflects your value. Refusing to devalue what was worth dying for. Friends, do you think of yourself as holy? Or, to continue the analogy, do you treat yourself or allow others to treat you like a used Starbucks cup?

It saddens me when I see women treat themselves as cheap and common when God says, "You are a treasured possession." Remember, we behave how we believe. Friends, your identity and my identity are holy. We are set apart for God. We are not common. Consequently we are to live our lives unto God and for His purposes.

Remember Who You Are

It is imperative that we remember our identity in Christ. We are immersed in a culture that demands that we conform to its norms and find our worth in its values. The battle for our minds is intense because from our thinking flows our actions and attitudes. To live as radiant women, we must daily choose to align our thoughts with God's truth and walk in the freedom that He bestows.

The Devil Wears Prada is a great example of how easily we are swayed and influenced by our surroundings. Andy Sachs, played by Anne Hathaway, begins working at *Runway* magazine for "the devil," Miranda Priestly, played by Meryl Streep. Initially Andy's goal is to have a career as a hard-hitting journalist, and the pressure of fitting the *Runway* image does not influence her. She jokes and laughs at the girls who are obsessed with being a size zero and whose lives revolve around pleasing the unappeasable Miranda. Over time, however, Andy changes. Lured by the desire for success and fearing the disappointment of her boss, she conforms into the image of a *Runway* girl. Her makeover leads her down a path of moral compromise and ultimately to conform to the image of a woman who she initially called the devil.

Each one of us, like Andy, lives and operates in a world that wants us to conform to darkness instead of living as radiant women. I write this to make you aware of the pull and prepared for the pressure. Your life has a glorious purpose and path before it. Don't be deceived and give in to the demands of darkness. Never forget, your eternal passport reads: Light of the World!

SHINE ON!

Do you long for radiance? Remember, the only one who has the right to define you is the One who created you . . . and Jesus says that you are worth dying for! Your identity reads: priceless treature!

Jesus Christ lived and died and rose in order to form the Holy People of God—a community of Christians who would live under the sway of the Spirit, men and women who would be human torches aglow with the fire of love for Christ, prophets and lovers ignited with the flaming Spirit of God.

Brennan Manning, *The Importance of Being Foolish*

CHAPTER FOUR

A Radiant Woman Is Connected to Her Power Source

Plugged In

After much deliberation, I decided my living room's theme would be "Texas chic." Or at least, that's how I described the look I was going for to my friend who volunteered to decorate. I suppose I should mention that I bought my first house this year. Yep, it's official . . . I'm a big girl now.

Girlfriends, let me just say for the record that I had no idea the amount of time, money, and effort it was going to take to get settled into my new place. Weeks after I moved, I was still living out of boxes, and the only furniture that I owned was from my college bedroom. No one warned me about the nesting gene that women have. I was completely unprepared for the phenomenon that would overcome me once I had my own house. All of a sudden, I needed, *desperately* needed, to watch the sundry of home improvement and decorating programs on television. Seriously, I was obsessed. Obsessed, broke, and did I mention living out of boxes?

If I'm honest, the television shows did more harm than good. They left me too overwhelmed with options to make a decision. Should each "space" be modern, classic, traditional, or contemporary? So many choices!!! The whole process of choosing paint colors, picking furniture, and deciding on one decorating style was more than I could handle. I found it strange that I had no problem committing to a thirty-year mortgage, but for the life of me, I couldn't commit to a sofa. I know. It's crazy.

I forgot to mention that I moved during one of my busiest ministry seasons. So even though I longed for my home to feel settled, I was at my wits' end as to how I could get it all done in the midst of traveling, speaking, and writing. Then God sent me a decorating "Angel." My precious friend (whose name happens to be Angel), sensing the dilemma that I was in, stepped in and said, "Just let me handle it. I'll get everything arranged and decorated for you."

Hallelujah!

The girl's got skills. She is supercreative and knows my personality so well. All she needed from me was a decorating theme. That's when the idea of "Texas chic" was born. I saw this photo of wild horses running and fell in love with the passion captured by the photographer, and I asked Angel to decorate my living room around that print.

So one day while I was away on a speaking engagement, my friend created her own version of the show "While You Were Out." While I was out, she and a few other friends performed the most amazing decorating transformation you can imagine. My living room went from feeling like a bland and boring asylum to fabulous Texas chic in a day.

Like I said, the girl's got skills. Everything is so "me" without "me" having to do the work. When I walked in for the "big reveal," I was truly blown away by all the hard work and little touches she had accomplished on such a small budget. She completely captured the theme without it feeling obnoxious or over the top. My favorite detail is a Texas star that she positioned atop my armoire. Decorators say that lighting is the key and I agree. The room looks its best when the lights are dim and only the star is shining bright.

A few days after the makeover, I realized another benefit to the star—it served as a fabulous night-light. Because I must walk through the living room to get to the kitchen at night, the star shines in the darkness so I can easily navigate around furniture.

However, one night I woke up and needed something to drink. I stumbled down the hall toward the kitchen, and entering the living room, I discovered it pitch black. The star wasn't shining. I couldn't see anything. Panic ensued. No, not because I'm afraid of the dark, but because I feared the star's light had permanently gone out. You see, Angel found the star in a clearance bin at Pottery Barn, so I knew I couldn't get another one and was anxious that my favorite decorating detail was broken.

Then it dawned on me . . . check the plug!

Yay! Decorating catastrophe averted. The star was simply unplugged from its power source. As I was plugging the cord into the outlet, I thought, *This is why so many Christians struggle to live as the light of Christ in the world—we aren't plugged into our power source. Although God called us to be lights in the darkness, we fail so often because we are unplugged and trying to shine in our own power.*

A Christian's power source is the Holy Spirit of God. God didn't just save us from our sin and give us eternal life; He also gave us the power to glorify Him. In order to understand how to stay plugged in, I will explain *who* the Holy Spirit is, *how* He empowers us to live the Christian life, and *what* two potential barriers often limit the Spirit's power.

The Power Source

> As the deer pants for streams of water,
> so my soul pants for you, O God.
> My soul thirsts for God, for the living God.
> (Ps. 42:1–2)

To best understand the Holy Spirit's role as our power source, we must return briefly to the heart of our faith: our desperate need for God. Psalm 42 clearly articulates the human condition. We thirst for God. *Thirst* is defined as: "painfully feeling the want of something, or to eagerly long for something."[2] Just as God created within each of us a thirst mechanism for water and a hunger mechanism for food, so He also placed with our souls a thirst for Him. We are created by Him and for Him.

Born into sin, we are separated from God and continually feel the want until this relationship is restored. Blaise Pascal famously said, "Man was created with a God-shaped hole in his soul that can only be filled by God Himself." To remedy this problem, Jesus, God Himself, stepped into creation, took on human flesh, and brought about the reconciliation of God and man through His sacrificial death.

During Jesus' earthly ministry, He addressed our fundamental problem and invited all thirsty souls to come to Him to find true life. He said, "If anyone thirsts, let him come to Me and drink. He who believes in Me, as the Scripture has said, out of his heart will flow rivers of living water" (John 7:37–38 NKJV).

The context of this statement was the annual Jewish Feast of Tabernacles. Each year, the Jewish people celebrated how the Lord had provided for their every need during their forty-year wilderness journey. As we would imagine, God providing water in a barren desert for millions of people was a pretty big deal. This was a joyful feast, rich with symbolism.

On the last and "greatest day of the feast," the High Priest led the people in a procession from the temple through Jerusalem to the pool of Siloam. Here he filled a pitcher with water, and the procession continued back to the temple—every step of the journey in complete silence. Then, amidst thousands of worshippers, the High Priest poured the water out onto the altar—an act of worship that acknowledged God alone as the source of life.

At that precise moment, Jesus stood, and said in a loud voice, "If anyone is thirsty, let him come to Me and drink" (you just gotta love Jesus; He's not subtle). There, in the midst of the pomp and pageantry of religion, He revealed that He was the fulfillment of the symbol. He alone *is* the Living Water that quenches the thirst of man.

In case you think the procession just carried on its merry way, think again. The entire city was silent when the Son of God shouted His message. His hearers did not miss Jesus' meaning. He had the audacity to claim equality with God and set Himself forth as the solution to humanity's greatest need. Don't let anyone ever tell you that Jesus never claimed to be God. He knew exactly *who* He was and *why* He was sent.

Jesus invites thirsty souls to "come and drink." To drink means to believe. Friends, this invitation is more than mere "head knowledge." To drink implies to experience, to trust, and to depend upon Him. When we come to Jesus and drink of the Living Water, we forsake other fountains, admitting that they will never truly satisfy. Trusting in Jesus for life is what it means to be a Christian.

Notice what Jesus said next: "'Whoever believes in me, as the Scripture has said, streams of living water will flow from within him.' By this he meant the Spirit, whom those who believed in him were later to receive" (John 7:38–39).

God recognizes that forgiveness of sin is not enough to cure the human condition; we need a new nature, with new desires and new ability, if we are to glorify Him. This new nature is the Holy Spirit of God living within us. Just as Jesus promised, whoever believes in Him receives His Spirit.

God knows that we can't live radiant lives without His power. As I tell women all the time, if we could glorify God on our own, then the cross wouldn't have been necessary and Jesus wouldn't have bothered to send us His Spirit. That's why the apostle Paul said in Colossians 1:27, it "is Christ in you, the hope of glory." Our only hope to live glorious lives comes through the power of God living in us.

> When Jesus said, "You are the light," we hear, "you are the light," and we think the light has to come from us. So we try to generate the light ourselves. After a few attempts, it should become obvious that we just don't have the power. But we keep trying anyway. The Scripture says, "In Him was life, and that life was the light of men." This is a massive principle to remember: The light comes only from the life—the life of Christ in us. —*Shine: Make Them Wonder What You've Got*, the Newsboys

Christianity is not a self-improvement religion in which one tries really hard to do better, to work harder, or to be good. A genuine follower of Jesus says, "I can't do it. I need Jesus and His Spirit working in me if I'm going to glorify God." Girls, we must come to the end of ourselves and recognize that we don't have the power to glorify God on our own. By faith, we believe in Jesus and He puts His Spirit within us, enabling us to shine brightly as lights in the darkness.

So, who is the Holy Spirit? The big theological answer is: He is the third person of the Triune God. The orthodox Christian belief concerning God is that He is one in essence yet three in persons: Father, Son, and Holy Spirit. Just as Jesus is fully God, so His Spirit is fully God. Why then, does God send us His Spirit? Professor of Theology Sinclair Ferguson explains:

> The Spirit's task is to restore glory to a fallen creation. As Calvin well says, this world was made theatre for God's glory. Throughout it (the world) he displays visibly the perfections of his invisible nature. Particularly in man and woman, his image, that glory was to be reflected. But they refused to "glorify" God (Rom. 1:21); they defiled the reflector (Rom. 1:28) and fell short of his glory (Rom. 3:23).
>
> But now, in Christ who is "the radiance of God's glory" (Heb. 1:3), that glory is restored. Now he sends his Spirit . . . to recover glory in us. So it is that "we, who with unveiled faces reflect the Lord's glory, are being transformed into his likeness with

ever-increasing glory, which comes from the Lord, who is the Spirit" (2 Cor. 3:18).

The purpose for which the Spirit is given is, therefore, nothing less than the reproduction of the image of God (in man.)[3]

I know. I know. I went really deep on you for a minute there. But, hang tight; this is good stuff. Definitely worth the brain power to read it again, but for those of us who live by *Cliffs Notes*, here's what we need to glean from that quote: **The Holy Spirit was sent to restore us to our original purpose by producing the radiance of Christ (God's glory) in us.** That's why He's our power source. Get it?

What absolutely blows my mind is the fact that the same Holy Spirit who raised Jesus from the dead, now lives in you and me. Wow—that is one powerful source! We are reminded of this truth in 1 Corinthians 3:16, when the apostle Paul says, "Don't you know that you yourselves are God's temple and that God's Spirit lives in you?" The Spirit living inside every believer is what Jesus foretold when He promised, "streams of living water will flow from within you."

Now that we understand who the Spirit is and that He lives within us, let's turn our attention to discover what the Holy Spirit does. After all, Jesus told us that it was to our advantage that He go away so that He could send us the Spirit (John 16:7). In other words, greater than having the Person of Christ standing before us is having the Spirit of Christ living within us.

How the Holy Spirit Produces Radiance

As we've seen, the Holy Spirit is our power source, producing Christlike character in us. We are completely dependent. But, what does this theology look like in daily life? Let's get practical: how can we live radiant lives?

The Bible teaches that radiance occurs when a life is under the control of and empowered by God's Spirit. Just as my Texas star must be filled with electricity in order to produce light, so we, too, must be "filled with the Spirit" if we are to shine.

The phrase "filled with the Spirit" is an expression taken from Ephesians 5:18, which says, "Do not get drunk on wine, which leads to debauchery. Instead, be filled with the Spirit." At first glance, this verse appears to be a simple command warning us against drunkenness.

If we carefully study the verse, we learn the secret to radiance: the Spirit-filled life. First, let's examine the Scripture in context to understand what Paul is teaching. For starters, he compares the filling of the Spirit with drunkenness. Please don't stop reading here and assume that those who are Spirit-filled are goofy and act like idiots. . . . This is NOT what this Scripture is teaching.

The comparison with drunkenness is given so we can understand the nature of influence. As you know, when a person is drunk (filled with alcohol), we say they are "under the influence." Back in my BC days (before Christ), I was often "under the influence." What does this mean? It means that my choices, words, actions, thoughts, and behaviors were *influenced* by alcohol (more than likely tequila, but that's beside the point).

The lesson is simple: **whatever fills us, controls us**. If we are filled with alcohol, we are controlled by (or under the influence of) alcohol. The same is true of the Spirit. If we are filled with the Spirit of God, then our lives are under the control of God; therefore, how we walk, talk, think, act, behave, etc., will be *influenced by Him.* The Holy Spirit will always influence us to live for God's glory. He perfectly fulfills the law of God by loving God and loving others.

Another way to understand this truth is to realize that the word *filled* in the Bible's original language describes a ship whose sail is filled with wind and carried along by the wind's power. Using this analogy, we are the ship and the Holy Spirit *fills* our sails and propels us to go in the direction that He desires.

This is how the Spirit produces radiance in us. He influences us to live according to God's will. He leads us to make choices that will shine a spotlight on Jesus. He empowers us to minister in His name and to love as Jesus loves.

Radiance! Remember . . . Jesus is the Radiant One, and it is His Life that causes us to be the Light of the World.

I can hear the question now, "But wait a minute, if this is true, then why is the church in such a mess? Why are we not more radiant? If, we have the power . . . then why isn't our light shining bright?"

The problem lies in radiant barriers.

Radiant Barriers

The guy seemed honest enough. Trust me, by this point I'd had enough plumbers, repair men, salesmen, and electricians in and out of the house to spot a con man a mile away and had received quite an education on all things plumbing, electrical, and flooring. My new home was not a money pit, per se, but it definitely proved to be more of a long-term investment than I had anticipated.

In the first few months of home ownership—after the superimportant detail of decorating was taken care of—I then turned my attention to home repair. YUCK! There is nothing worse in my opinion. I never disliked singleness more than I did when some shady repairman gave me an overpriced estimate because he thought he could pull one over on the single girl.

But, like I said, this guy seemed honest enough. My current problem was the house temperature. Downstairs . . . perfect. As Goldie Locks would say, "Just right!" But upstairs, where my precious roomies live, . . . not so perfect. It was an inferno of mythic proportions. Epic heat. Literally, there was a twenty-five-degree temperature difference between upstairs and downstairs.

So began the litany of repairmen, in and out of the house, all trying to solve my problem. Some said, "Ma'am, it's a vent problem." Others said, "Nope, honey, what you need is more insulation." But not this guy. . . . No, he showed up with his fancy flowcharts and graphs and said, "What you need to do is buy some radiant barrier." Radiant barrier? (I thought, *Is this a trick? Does he know I'm writing a book called* Radiant?) He had my full attention now. Snapping my head up from his slick flowchart, I looked him square in the eyes, and said, "Oh *really*, and what exactly is 'radiant barrier'?" He kind of chuckled and said, "It's a material we put on your roof to keep the light out."

AHA! Radiant barrier keeps the light out!

Let me just pause and say, as a writer and teacher of God's Word, I absolutely adore the moments when God delivers the perfect illustration on a silver platter. This is one of those times. I could have kissed the salesman, I was so happy. Bing!!! The lightbulb went on. What a perfect explanation as to why Christians, who have the Spirit of God, aren't living as lights in the darkness. We have our own radiant barriers that keep the light out—blocking the glory of God in our lives.

To understand our own radiant barriers, I want to recall how Jesus described the presence of the Spirit in our lives. Do you remember? He compared the Spirit to a "river of living water." If you've ever been white-water rafting, you have a good idea of what Jesus meant by "living water." This isn't a little creek or stream. His word picture brings to mind a mighty rushing river, full of power, surging down from a mountain, giving life to the valley below.

Changing metaphors from electricity to water, the rushing river is the image I want you to have of the Spirit's power in you. He is powerful. He is life-giving. He is refreshing. Now, as we explore the radiant barriers, we will do so by imagining types of blockades that hinder the river's flow.

Radiant Barrier #1—The Unsurrendered Will

The first radiant barrier we must tear down is an unsurrendered will. The human will is the place of decision. God created us with a free will, thus giving us the ability to choose. He did not create us to be robots with a preprogrammed function called "worship God" or an automatic pilot setting called "obedience." No, God gave us as His image bearers the ability to choose whether or not we would love, worship, and glorify Him.

I know it would have been so much easier if He had wired us that way, but look at it from God's perspective. If you created the world and its inhabitants out of love, then wouldn't it make sense that those creatures would choose to love you in return? If love isn't a choice, then is it really love? No, we call that a duty. No girl wants her boyfriend sending her flowers on Valentine's Day because it is his "duty." No, she wants the desire of his heart to be showing her how much he adores her. Big difference. God is most glorified when we (His creatures) choose to love and worship Him out of the freedom of our hearts because we recognize how worthy He is of our affection and devotion.

At some point every woman comes to the place where she decides whether or not she will surrender her life to the Lordship of Jesus Christ. Let's logically think about this one: Jesus is God. (check) The Bible tells us that He spoke the world into existence and sustains it by His power. (check) The only reason we can take our next breath is because He wills that it be so. (check) Yet, somehow, in our Christian vocabulary, we've created this expression: "*I* decided to make Jesus Lord of my life."

Let's get one thing straight. He is Lord . . . of everyone's life. That's not up for debate. As Philippians 2:10–11 so powerfully states, "at the name of Jesus every knee should bow, in heaven and on earth and under the earth, and every tongue confess that Jesus Christ is Lord, to the glory of God the Father." As the Scripture says, every knee *will* bow, so the question on the table is whether or not we will bow our knee and surrender to His Lordship willingly.

Choosing to love and glorify God is where the human will comes into play. The Bible teaches no one can say Jesus is Lord apart from the Holy Spirit. The Spirit helps us to recognize who God is and that we owe Him our lives and allegiance. Yet, even after we are new creations, our old pesky sinful nature rears its ugly head and resists God's authority by insisting, "Nope. I don't want to follow God. I want to do my own thing." When that unsurrendered attitude surfaces, a dam is erected across the river, causing the flow of the Spirit to come to a crushing halt.

Unbelief in the goodness and faithfulness of God causes an unsurrendered will, creating a dam that blocks the flow of God's Spirit. Looking back over my own life, I see how life-changing surrender was in my walk with God. I grew up in a Christian home and was raised attending church; I knew the facts concerning Christianity: Jesus was the Son of God who died for the sins of the world. The Bible tells us that the "demons know this and they shudder." Knowing that information did not transform my life. There is a big difference between knowing information and placing faith in Jesus. It wasn't until I was in my midtwenties and facing the reality that my life was in shambles that I realized that I needed God.

Trusting in Christ for salvation was amazing. He loved me, forgave me, healed me, and accepted me. But surrendering my will, laying down my agenda, choosing to live God's way instead of my own—now that took a little more work. There was a big problem. My heart didn't fully trust Him. I struggled to believe that God's plan and ways were better than my own. This is the issue for many people. Although we are grateful for salvation and pretty pumped about that whole eternity-in-heaven gig, when it comes down to who will run the show in our lives, well, that's crossing the line.

God leads, speaks, guides, and directs us, but if we aren't willing to follow, then our lives will not reflect the radiance of Christ. His life *is* in us, but when we resist Him, our lives don't produce the fruit of the Spirit. Remember, whatever fills you, controls you, and the only way the Spirit controls us is if we choose to place ourselves under His influence.

Dr. Henry Cloud and Dr. John Townsend explain how surrendering to the Spirit works in their book *How People Grow*:

> Often in the growth process we do not know what
> to do, or we do not want to do what we know we
> should do. This is where the "control" of the Spirit

comes into play, and we must yield. We must submit to what the Holy Spirit is telling us to do and
allow him to have the reins of control moment by
moment.

The moment-by-moment task is not only one
of asking, but of being filled with his power and
of yielding to his control. The Holy Spirit talks to
us, brings to mind things God has said, shows us
a way out, gives us answers, gives us things to say,
and pushes us to take a risk. But when he nudges or
reminds, *our job is to yield to him and allow him to
have control. We are to submit and yield our will.* In
that way, he takes us where we need to go.[4]

Each act of obedience in the life of a Christian is a step of surrender. Yielding says yes to the Lordship of Jesus and no to our
flesh. Surrender acknowledges that He is God and knows far
better how our lives should go than we do. It is an act of trust
and a step of love to believe that God's ways are good and He
has our best interests at heart.

My life changed the day I fell in love with Jesus. When
God opened my eyes to see His glory and majesty, my heart
responded with love. This love resulted in a deeper trust that
propelled me to surrender my will to God's will.

I keep a quote by Nancy Leigh DeMoss posted above
my desk as a daily reminder of why I should surrender to the
Spirit's promptings. It says "Obedience is a willing, glad-hearted

response to the God who loves us extravagantly and has our best interest at heart."⁵ Her words remind me that the *why* of surrender is love. I know God loves me and desires good for me; therefore, I choose to yield to His will.

The Holy Spirit has been faithful to reveal areas in my life that are still not surrendered. I'm still in the process—learning to surrender every area of my life to the lordship of Jesus Christ by allowing His spirit to "influence" and "direct" me along the way.

What's blocking the light of Christ in your life? What area is still not surrendered to His lordship? Jesus said a "bad tree produces bad fruit." One way to determine if we are surrendered to the Lord is to examine the fruit in our lives. Are we producing the fruit of the Spirit, or do we find pride, anger, lust, jealousy, and greed growing instead? These are fruits of the sinful nature and are evidence that the Spirit of God is not flowing.

Friends, from one follower of Jesus to another, let me encourage you—surrender! Saying yes to Jesus when He speaks and submitting to His will produce the most beautiful bounty of blessings. I urge you to ask the Holy Spirit to show you any "dam" that is blocking His flow and, right now, get on your knees and allow the dynamite of God's love to tear it down. Believe, sweet sisters, His will is good.

> Therefore, I urge you, brothers, **in view of God's mercy**, to **offer** your bodies as living sacrifices, holy and pleasing to God—this is your spiritual act of

worship. Do not conform any longer to the pattern of this world, but be transformed by the renewing of your mind. Then you will be able to test and approve what **God's will is—his good, pleasing and perfect will**. (Rom. 12:1–2, emphasis added)

Radiant Barrier #2—Unconfessed Sin

In order to understand the second radiant barrier that blocks the Spirit's power, think back with me to our river analogy. Imagine that the mighty rushing river becomes polluted. Instead of pure, crystal-clear flowing water, it becomes grossly littered with trash and debris. How did this happen? First, someone discarded an empty Coke can into the river. Sure, she may have felt a tinge of guilt the first time, but soon it became easy to toss in one after another. A few weeks pass by, and she decides that the river is the perfect place to discard an old tire and then the next month rationalizes dumping a bunch of household trash. Eventually all of this trash builds up downstream, blocking the flow and causing the river to slow to a trickle.

This illustration shows how unconfessed sin can work in a Christian's life. Sin is the debris that blocks the radiance of Christ from being seen in us. Even though the Holy Spirit is always present in a believer, when we choose to sin and not deal with it, the Spirit's flow (His fruit, life, and power) slows to a trickle.

Sin is defined as falling short of the glory of God. This means that there is a standard—God's perfect holiness—and when we miss that standard (sin), we do not glorify God with our lives. Translation: we are not living radiantly.[6] This begs the question: what do we do with the sin that we still battle on a daily basis?

We deal with sin by *confessing* it and allowing God to *cleanse* it from our lives. Confession means to acknowledge the sin. In other words, we admit that there is trash in the river.

> This is the message we have heard from him and declare to you: God is light; in him there is no darkness at all. If we claim to have fellowship with him yet walk in the darkness, we lie and do not live by the truth.
>
> But if we walk in the light, as he is in the light, we have fellowship with one another, and the blood of Jesus, his Son, purifies us from all sin.
>
> If we claim to be without sin, we deceive ourselves and the truth is not in us. **If we confess our sins**, he is faithful and just and will forgive our sins and **purify us** from all unrighteousness. (1 John 1:5–9, emphasis added)

Here's the problem: instead of confessing our sin to God and allowing Him to cleanse us, many times we choose to ignore it, to deny it, or even to blame it on others. All of these options leave us with a big problem: the radiant barrier of unconfessed sin.

If we don't deal with sin immediately, we "grieve the Holy

Spirit" (Eph. 4:30), and our fellowship with God is hindered. Why? Sin grieves the heart of God because it pollutes us and it is rebellion, which at the core means we don't trust Him. This brings us back to the heart of radiance: love. When we love Jesus, we want the world to see that we trust Him and by our obedience we testify that He is good.

If we desire to live radiant lives, we must clear out the junk and the trash that pollutes us. We start by taking an honest self-examination and asking the Holy Spirit to search our hearts (Ps. 139:23–24). Confess any sin that is revealed and receive the forgiveness Jesus offers. Once we do this, our fellowship with God is renewed and His Spirit flows unhindered.

Allow me to share how this works in my own life. I recognize that I'm not producing the fruit of the Spirit (love, joy, peace, patience, etc.). Additionally, I experience an uneasy feeling or a lack of peace, which tips me off that I've grieved the Spirit. For example, suppose I say something in conversation that is hurtful to the other person. I will sense I've displeased the Lord, and the Holy Spirit will tug at my heart until I confess the sin. Keep in mind that the Christian life is a relationship. I must choose to surrender and walk in obedience *because* I love Jesus and want His glorious light seen in my life.

Some days I remedy the problem quickly; other times I choose to ignore God's voice, and the nagging feeling may last for longer periods. But eventually, I ask God, "What is blocking Your Spirit?" Then, through prayer or reading the Word, God reveals the unconfessed sin, such as gossip, pride, anger, envy, or jealousy—bringing to mind the incident or the true motive behind it.

When I see my sin, own up to it, and take it to Jesus, I receive both grace and cleansing. Once I've confessed, I sense the life of the Spirit flowing through me again—renewing the joy, the peace, and the love of God, which are unmistakable.

Over the years I've learned to keep short accounts with God. This means I try to confess sin quickly without it building up and blocking the Spirit's flow. Girls, I don't want to go too long without His power—that is a disaster waiting to happen. For that reason, I pray for a heart sensitive to God's leading and that I would be easy to discipline and quick to convict. When I sin, I don't want to just ignore it because I know over time my heart will grow hard and insensitive to His voice. Therefore, I try to confess sin when it happens or as soon as God reveals it so that I can experience the joy and freedom of unhindered fellowship with God.

I hope this explanation is helpful. God gives us the power to live radiant lives through His Spirit; our only job is to remove any barriers that stand in His way.

Just Say No to Sharpay

I'm singing out loud at the top of my lungs as I write these words . . . you'll understand why in a few minutes. This summer I had the joy of speaking to a group of elementary-aged girls at a summer camp. Since I normally don't teach girls younger than college age, I felt unprepared to communicate. Honestly, I don't know the first thing about ten-year-olds. I don't even remember what I was like back then, and heaven knows that times have changed.

So a friend of mine suggested I watch the *High School Musical* movies. She said, and she was so right, that "little girls love *HSM*!" So, one Saturday I devoted the entire day to developing a Zac Efron crush. Ooooo, he's so cute. I know. I'm pathetic. Don't judge.

Watching these movies, one quickly realizes that the nemesis of the show is a character named Sharpay. She puts the drama in "drama queen." Her life ambition is to be a star, and she will do whatever it takes to achieve her goal.

In *HSM3* (as we fans like to call it) Sharpay is up to her old tricks and is determined to win a coveted spot in a New York City drama school. Sharpay makes her purpose known when she stands on stage, in the middle of her high school auditorium and proclaims, "I want it all. Center-stage with the spotlight on ME!"

Ruthless and cutthroat, Sharpay manipulates others to get her way. Lying, cheating, and deceiving are but mere child's play for this young woman on a mission. As I watched Sharpay, I couldn't help thinking how very similar she is to humanity apart from God's Spirit working in us. Our sinful nature (the flesh) is focused on ourselves and determined to get our own way. It really doesn't give a rip about the glory of God; it is too busy trying to get center-stage for itself. And frankly, it is kind of perturbed that God would have the audacity to think that this world is about *Him*.

Sure, it's human nature. But, it's not God's nature. When the Spirit of God comes to dwell in us, we have a new nature and a new desire. We want Jesus to be applauded, lifted up, and exalted. He is the Famous One whose praise we live to proclaim. Of course, there is a battle between our old sinful nature and the Spirit of God living in us; but each time we say yes to the Spirit, we overcome the flesh—fulfilling our purpose of glorifying God.

The Holy Spirit will always shine the spotlight on Jesus. This serves as a good litmus test for our lives. We can know if we are under the Spirit's influence by whether or not our lives are bringing Jesus glory. Radiant women, let us say no to the Sharpay that's still living in us. Now say yes to the Holy Spirit whose driving ambition is to exalt Jesus Christ.

Now, instead of singing with Sharpay, "I Want It All," the song that spills forth from our radiant souls is one of praise and adoration to our great God! Go ahead and take a minute to sing the chorus to a worship song that you know by heart. If you can't think of one, download "Famous One" by Chris Tomlin and belt out the lyrics to this great affirmation of our great God. Sing it like you mean it!

AND . . . after you sing a couple rounds, take a minute and bounce back to the appendix. I've included a handy summary of the Holy Spirit's work in a Christian's life that you'll definitely want to check out.

SHINE ON!
Pray through each of the radiant barriers; asking the
Holy Spirit to flood through your life.

You were once darkness, but now you are light in the Lord.
Live as children of light.

Ephesians 5:8

CHAPTER FIVE

A Radiant Woman Knows "What Not to Wear"

I have a precious friend who absolutely means the world to me. The thing I love best about her is the fact that she is 100 percent herself, comfortable in her own skin. She's a girl who is so laid-back that others feel at ease in her presence and she doesn't have a pretentious bone in her body. Due to this high level of self-comfort, my friend is not hyperconcerned about keeping up with the latest fashion trends or dressing to impress others . . . although she never fails to look beautiful, she's just all about low maintenance, comfort clothing.

Comfortable jeans, comfortable bras, comfortable dresses, COMFORT is her fashion statement. My friend is known for her famous fleece pants. These are famous because we affectionately call them the "dog pants." You see, my friend has a rather large dog whose hair sticks to her favorite fleece pants like teenyboppers to Zac Efron. She has been known to visit Starbucks, the grocery store, and occasionally a movie theater in her favorite pair of fleece. You guessed it; her rationale is, "but they are so comfortable!"

One day I sweetly mentioned to my friend that I was going to nominate her for the show "What Not to Wear" on TLC. Although I love the fact that she lives in freedom and doesn't worship the gods of Prada, Armani, and *Vogue*, I thought we might need professional help to intervene and rip the dog pants out of her life for good.

I'm just sayin' . . . dog hair? That's where I draw the line.

Unbeknownst to me, another friend of hers wanted to nominate her for the show as well. This fact was revealed while they were chatting on the phone about their upcoming sorority pledge-class reunion. My friend, who will be called "Dog Pants" or DP for short, was a little wigged out because she knew her comfort clothes weren't going to cut it with all the fashion divas. Therefore, DP had called up her friend the fashion expert and asked for her advice on her clothing for the dinner.

DP has quite an illustrative vocabulary, so she took painstaking effort to describe the outfit she would wear to dinner. She described the dress (the length, the cut, the color) and the jewelry (size, color, shape, matching pieces). Then finally, she said, "And I thought I'd wear my *dressy* flip flops." DP tried to continue on, but her friend interrupted, "What do you mean by 'dressy flip flops'?"

DP said, "Well, they are black . . . with the thingy that goes between my toes, and they're super comfortable—" At that last statement, her friend interrupted again and said, "Do you mean *pool* shoes?" To which DP responded, "Sure, I guess you could wear them to the pool." But before she could finish, her fashion advisor leveled her final question: "If you threw them in the pool . . . would they float?"

What *Not* to Wear

All of us need fashion advice now and again. I think that's the reason the show "What Not to Wear" on TLC is so popular. The premise of the program is this: the hosts surprise a fashion victim in her hometown, explain to said victim why her friends and family think she's a prime candidate for their services, show her videotaped evidence of her fashion crimes, and then collect her entire wardrobe and whisk her off to New York City for an in-depth fashion makeover.

Once in New York, the fashion victim is thrust before the most awful mirrors in human history. These ghastly full-length, all-direction mirrors expose every lump and flaw. And girls, don't even get me started on the lighting . . . or should I say, "cellulighting." I think they choose the worst fluorescent light possible in order to sway the fashion victim to their side. After the poor girl has been exposed for the fashion disaster that she is, the two stylists explain *why* her previous look wasn't working and *what* she should wear in the future.

As I've thought about this show, I've discovered many parallels to the Christian life. Namely, a key factor in radiance is found in our understanding "what not to wear." Just as the reformed style offender in the television program, a radiant woman knows that there are certain actions, attitudes, and behaviors that she should take off and others that she should put on.

In the Bible, clothing often represents a person's identity, role, or calling. For instance, the priest in the Old Testament wore specific garments, as did the kings. Also, unmarried women (virgins) were easily recognized because they wore beautiful robes that symbolized their purity. In the Hebrew culture, clothing was representative of the character and identity of the wearers.

Wardrobe Change

A spiritual wardrobe change is a major theme of the New Testament. The apostle Paul, when explaining the new nature and lifestyle of a follower of Jesus, uses the illustration of a person changing clothing as a metaphor for the process of our spiritual transformation.

In Romans 13, Paul carefully illustrates how a follower of Jesus undergoes a spiritual wardrobe change. He begins his argument by calling our attention to the fact that we are no longer citizens of darkness (as we discussed in chapter 2), but we are citizens of the kingdom of light . . . and with this change of residence comes a change of wardrobe.

> Wake up, for our salvation is nearer now than when we first believed. The night is almost gone; the day of salvation will soon be here. So remove your dark deeds like dirty clothes, and put on the shining armor of right living. Because we belong to the day, we must live decent lives for all to see. Don't participate in the darkness of wild parties and drunkenness, or in sexual promiscuity and immoral living, or in quarreling and jealousy. Instead, clothe yourself with the presence of the Lord Jesus Christ. And don't let yourself think about ways to indulge your evil desires. (Rom. 13:11–14 NLT)

One thing I'd like to clarify from the start is *why* we undergo this wardrobe change. It is not an attempt to earn our salvation or to make us acceptable before God. Actually, it is the opposite. The reason we change our clothes is because we *are* now different people, new creations in Christ—complete with new clothing that reflects this new identity.

For example, I remember watching a reality TV show about the Dallas Cowboys's cheerleaders. One thing I remember about watching the tryouts—aside from my gratitude that I did not pursue that childhood fantasy—was that it was only *after* a girl officially made the squad that she received her uniform. She was named a cheerleader first, and her clothing was then an assumed part of the position.

As Christians we don't need to earn a spot on God's team; Jesus earned that for us. He lived the perfect, sinless life and then died for our sins. By faith in Him, we are declared righteous before God and receive all the benefits that belong to His child. Now that we are "on God's team," so to speak, we *do* get a new wardrobe *because* of our status, not our performance. We are robed in the very radiance of Christ. But, there's a big problem. So many of us choose to live in our old, ragged, worn-out, smelly "deeds of darkness" rather than put on the radiance of Christ.

Off with the Old

> You were taught, with regard to your former way of life, to put off your old self, which is being corrupted by its deceitful desires; to be made new in the attitude of your minds; and to put on the new self, created to be like God in true righteousness and holiness. (Eph. 4:22–24)

Let's examine a little more specifically what we should "put off," or what the Bible says we ought not to wear. Romans 13:13 describes this old wardrobe as wild parties and drunkenness, sexual promiscuity and immoral living, and quarreling and jealousy. Sounds like an episode of *Gossip Girls*, huh? These attitudes and activities are normal for someone who is still "living in darkness," but they are unacceptable for a child of God who is called to reflect the very radiance of Christ to the world.

But why?

Are we just being legalistic and prudish here? No ma'am! I don't think so at all. Trust me, I realize these activities are glamorized by our culture and made to seem the norm for any young woman. I've experienced the heartbreak that comes from buying into this lie. After the glitz of the *Gossip Girls* nightlife are mornings filled with insecurity and regret, and heartbreak and shame litter the floor like the quickly removed garments from the previous evening. I know why a radiant woman does not want to put those clothes back on . . . the taint of the mistakes lingers long after the smoky smell fades.

God calls us to put off these activities because Jesus died to rescue us from darkness. Walking in the light of Christ is far better, but if we choose to remain in and participate in the old deeds of darkness, we will miss out on all that God has in store for us. Jesus said, "I have come that [you] may have life and have it in abundance" (John 10:10 HCSB). The problem with the party scene and wild, promiscuous lifestyle is that we seek to find fulfillment in things that will never satisfy. The ways of darkness will ultimately leave us empty.

As I've mentioned, I know this one from experience. Jesus rescued me from the deeds of darkness. I wore wild parties, drunkenness, and sexual sin like a tight-fitting pair of daisy dukes. So, when Christ set me free from "looking for love in hookups, happy hour, and hangovers," my spiritual wardrobe needed to undergo a serious transformation (as did my physical wardrobe, but that's a whole different lesson). I had to learn what not to wear. I had to take off those old behaviors and to "put on" Jesus. Let me just say, I'm so very glad that I did. That old lifestyle seemed fun for a moment, but it led me down a path of destruction and heartache. The buzz eventually became a hangover, the hookup always led to a walk of shame, and the happy hour just stopped making me happy after a while.

Jesus is right. He *is* life. Today, I have joy . . . unspeakable joy. I am filled with His life and instead of feeling used, devalued, and empty . . . I feel free, alive, and loved. It's just common sense to me that the God who loves us so lavishly would want us to put off behaviors and attitudes that ultimately hurt and destroy us. He says to take off sexual immorality because sexual sin is destructive to our bodies, minds, souls, and spirits. Jesus loves us too much to just sit back and watch us destroy ourselves.

I've found that it was so much easier for me to burn those old "clothes of darkness" when I understood God's heart. He wants so much *better* for me—and you. God isn't anti-sex. Don't let anyone lie to you. God created sex, and He designed it to bless us; but like the rest of God's creation, sex only works according to His design. One man. One woman. In a covenant called marriage. Anything outside of God's perfect design will leave us empty and hurting.[7]

God loves us. As a result, He wants us take off anything that isn't His best for us. For example, God knows that drunkenness is just our vain attempt to fill our emptiness with alcohol. It doesn't matter how many shots we throw back or how many cocktails we pour, we wake up the next day, the same person with the same problems. The ramifications of drunkenness are poor choices, dulled senses, and potential addiction. The true filling that we long for is found only in Christ. Hence, we are to put off drunkenness because it is just *so* last season. And let's face it: the behaviors that come with drunkenness don't reflect the radiance of Christ to the world.

Don't assume darkness is limited to the proverbial "drugs, sex, and rock-n-roll" because that is far from the case. A person could live an extremely dark and godless life and never taste a sip of alcohol or indulge in the activities described above. The essence of darkness is a life without God and a life centered on self. The manifestations of the flesh are not limited to drunkenness and sexual sin, but rather they are numerous, as Paul describes in Galatians 5:19–21: *"When you follow the desires of your sinful nature, the results are very clear: sexual immorality, impurity, lustful pleasures, idolatry, sorcery, hostility, quarreling, jealousy, outbursts of anger, selfish ambition, dissension, division, envy, drunkenness, wild parties, and other sins like these. Let me tell you again, as I have before, that anyone living that sort of life will not inherit the Kingdom of God"* (NLT).

According to our focal passage in Romans 13, the other deed of darkness that we are called to remove regards our interpersonal relationships—jealousy and quarreling. *Mean Girls* might have been a funny movie, but it is a horrible way to live. Jealousy and quarreling are unfashionable for a radiant woman because they don't reflect the nature and character of Jesus. Our old nature was focused on seeking the best for self, but the character of Christ is the opposite—it's all about seeking the best for others.

We no longer live as the rest of the world lives in its backstabbing, gossip, and hatred. Instead, radiant women should take off selfishness, pride, and anything that causes jealousy and fighting with one another. We have a new ambition now: we live to shine the spotlight on the face of Jesus, and we want the world to see a transformed life at our "big reveal."

No Provision

> Put on the Lord Jesus Christ, and make no provision
> for the flesh. (Rom. 13:14 NASB)

I hope you are getting the mental picture the Bible is painting for us. Just as a woman goes through her closet and removes outdated and unfitting clothing, we are to throw out attitudes and behaviors that don't reflect the radiance of Christ. That old wardrobe that we throw out is often referred to as the deeds of the flesh. Now, "flesh" is just a biblical term for our old sinful nature. You know, that thing in each of us that still wants to sin, rebel against God, and do our own thing. We've all got flesh.

And as we talked about in the previous chapter, we overcome the flesh when we surrender to the influence of the Holy Spirit.

Romans chapter 13 gives us a great warning concerning the flesh in the context of how we change our wardrobe. It says that we are to "make no provision" for the flesh and its desires. What in the world does that mean? I was studying this passage and decided to research the word *provision*. Once I understood the meaning, Paul's warning hit me straight between the eyes. The definition of *provision* is "to prepare ahead of time."

Provision . . .

Recently I went to speak at a girls' camp in the middle of Texas. Because I was going to be driving for a day and doing many camp activities upon arrival, I made certain provisions for my trip. Such as, buying road trip snacks, packing for a week away from home, renting a book on CD for the drive, and making sure someone would check my mail while I was out of town.

Provision . . .

Now, when the Bible says "make no provision for the flesh," it is teaching us to avoid setting ourselves up for sinful behaviors or placing ourselves in situations when we will be extremely tempted to wear the old deeds of darkness *if ya know what I mean*. Basically, when we talk about making no provision for the flesh, we are choosing to not place ourselves in situations where our flesh will get in trouble or we set ourselves up for failure.

Here are a few examples:

- If I struggle with alcohol and drunkenness, then hanging out in a bar would "make provision" for my flesh.
- If I struggle with gossip, then hanging out with my girlfriends who love to spread the latest rumor or trash people behind their backs would "make provision" for my flesh.
- If I'm a married woman, then venting about my husband to my cute male coworker and spending time with him outside of work is "making provision" for the flesh.
- If I'm a single woman and desire to remain sexually pure in my dating life, then I should not spend time alone, in the dark, with the guy I'm dating (even if I'm telling myself we're just going to watch a movie on the couch). That choice is just setting us both up for failure . . . and is definitely making provision for the flesh.

Let me be clear. The reason God wants us to put off the deeds of darkness and make no provision for the flesh is for our own good. This command is calling us to not be cavalier about sin and its consequences. If we're going to be radiant, we can't be flippant and think, *It's just no big deal. I can handle it. It's not going to affect me.*

Countless Christian women have told me heartbreaking

stories of alcohol-induced sexual sin, unplanned pregnancies, accidental addictions, and friendships ruined by gossip all because the warning was not heeded against making provision for the flesh. Girls, we've got to wake up and understand that there is a deceptive power that despises our glow. Our enemy would love for us to live in the darkness and never reflect the light of Christ to the world.

Therefore, we must make no provision. That may mean we need to make some tough choices, and we will definitely need accountability with certain struggles. Just today a friend called to ask that I would hold her accountable in her dating life. She loves Jesus and wants to honor Him by remaining sexually pure until marriage, so she asked me to help her set up boundaries and hold her accountable to them. This means I have the freedom to ask tough questions, and she will call me if she is tempted to put on that old wardrobe.

Having an accountability partner is like that friend who joins you to shop and who will tell you the flat-out truth even when it hurts. This is the friend who wouldn't dare let you walk out of the store in an outfit that made you look like one of the girls with the black bar across her eyes on the back page of *Glamour* magazine.

I've been blessed with the same accountability group for a few years now. These girls know my junk. I tell them my struggles, and they share theirs with me. Together we help one another "make no provision for the flesh" through prayer and by encouraging one another to make radiant choices.

If you are struggling to take off the old sinful nature and put on the radiance of Christ, find a few close girlfriends who also love Jesus and who desire to be radiant women. Make a plan to meet regularly, study God's Word, pray together, and encourage each other in your Christ-honoring choices.

What's a Girl to Wear?

> Put aside the deeds of darkness and *put on the armor of light*. (Rom. 13:12)

"What am I going to wear?" is perhaps one of the most often repeated female questions of all time. I know I ask myself the question just about every morning of my life. And if the occasion is big, I ask others and myself this question multiple times. And I might just start obsessing about what to wear days, if not weeks, in advance.

What we wear is a big deal, is it not?

Just as we take time to think through what we put on our bodies, a radiant woman is not one who just runs out the door each morning without getting spiritually dressed. She knows what to wear and chooses to clothe herself in the wardrobe befitting the radiance of Christ.

My favorite segment of *What Not to Wear* is when the fashion experts take their protégé aside and teach her the looks and styles that work best for her body type and personal activities. With much enthusiasm, they explain the blessing of an a-line skirt for girls with wider hips and the elongating benefits of a good v-neck top. Thankfully the Bible does the same for you and for me. Once we've removed the deeds of darkness, we clothe ourselves in the radiance of Christ. Scripture teaches us the three key garments that we should wear:

1. Love,
2. Life-giving words,
3. and Humility.

Put on Love

> Therefore, as God's chosen people, holy and dearly loved, clothe yourselves with compassion, kindness, humility, gentleness and patience. Bear with each other and forgive whatever grievances you may have against one another. Forgive as the Lord forgave you. And over all these virtues put on love, which binds them all together in perfect unity. (Col. 3:12–14)

Have you ever heard the expression "dress the part"? The meaning behind the phrase is that we wear the wardrobe appropriate for the role or the position that we desire. I think that is good advice for the Christian life. Nothing reveals the character of Christ more to the world than sacrificial love. Love is seeking the best for another—to put someone else first.

We live and operate in a world that is focused on self. Because everyone is looking out for #1, nothing stands out more than when a Christian woman intentionally chooses to "put on love." Our light becomes a stark contrast to the darkness of anger, hatred, and selfishness. Once again, it is only by His power that we are able to truly love as He loves. Notice the reason we change our wardrobe: the text tells us because we are "holy and dearly loved," we put on a wardrobe that matches our new identity. *Are you seeing how these truths work together: Purpose+ Identity+ Power= Radiance.*

One thing I've noticed over the years is that the most unkind and unloving people are those who are hurting the most inside. Hurt people hurt people. Deep within their hearts they don't feel accepted or loved; their treatment of others reflects the contempt and alienation they feel. That is precisely why Christians should be the most loving people on earth: deep within our hearts we realize we *are* unconditionally accepted.

God speaks His love over us and invites us into a relationship with Him where we are showered with love and grace. As a result of this downpour of acceptance, our hearts are free to love others. If you are thinking, *If that is true, then why aren't Christians more loving?* I totally agree and propose two reasons: the first is an issue of *belief,* and the second is an issue of *battle.*

Belief. The fundamental doctrine of the Christian faith is: Jesus died to pay the penalty for our sins; by faith in Him, we are made right before God. While that is the crux of our faith, actually believing this truth to the point that it transforms your heart is an entirely different matter.

My pastor and friend, Ben Young, often says, "We must

preach the gospel to ourselves every single day." The reason? Not because we can lose our salvation but because we are so extremely forgetful. We forget that we are accepted not by our works or good behavior, but rather 100 percent because of Jesus' sacrificial death. The consequence of our forgetfulness allows us to fall back into works-based living with the resulting feelings of shame and condemnation. When our hearts don't feel love and acceptance, we don't extend love and acceptance to others. If we are to love, truly love, we must receive God's love. We cannot give what we do not have.

Battle. The daily battle with the flesh impedes our ability to love. By now, we should have a pretty good grasp of what the flesh is. If not, just think, *selfishness.* Selfishness is the opposite of love because it puts the needs of self above others. The battle between the flesh and the Spirit of God within us is an ongoing fight. Yet, the more we surrender to God, the more we, in turn, are led by the Spirit. How does this apply to love?

As we know, there are some people who are easier to love, and there are some situations in which it is easier to show love. We inevitably find ourselves immersed in difficult moments when our flesh yearns to get even, to yell at another driver, to ignore someone in need, to spit out a snide remark, **but then** . . . God's Spirit in us desires to extend love, so we rein in our flesh and let the Spirit lead.

Yes, we can actually love people even when we don't feel like loving people. C. S. Lewis, commenting on the command to put on love, remarked:

Do not waste time bothering whether you 'love' your neighbor; act as if you did. As soon as we do this we find one of the great secrets. When you are behaving as if you loved someone, you will presently come to love him. If you injure someone you dislike, you will find yourself disliking him more. If you do him a good turn you will find yourself disliking him less.[8]

I've found Lewis's words to be great advice. Essentially, he's telling us to "fake it until we make it." If I choose in the morning to get up and put on love, just like today I chose to put on jeans and a T-shirt, then I will be conscious of God's heart and will remember to ask for His power to love the people He chooses to place in my path.

Put on Life-Giving Words

"Sticks and stones may break my bones, but words will never harm me." Pardon my frankness, but that's absolute garbage! Words hurt. I have scars on my body from scrapes and falls of all sorts, the cause for which I can't recall, but I can easily remember with vivid accuracy the setting, scene, and sequence of events when hurtful and heartbreaking words were spoken. Words are powerful. Long after physical wounds heal, the emotional wounds that result from our words linger on. As Proverbs 18:21 reminds us, *life and death are in the power of the tongue.*

Let me be honest and say that I shudder with regret over words that I've spoken in the past. With my impetuous and spontaneous personality, I've been prone to speak long before my little brain had time to think. As a result, I've hurt some feelings along the way. Now that I love Jesus, I hate knowing that I hurt anyone—intentionally or unintentionally. I know we all have said things that we wish we hadn't said. Jesus and I are working on this issue . . . daily. One thing I've learned is the importance of coming to Him in prayer every morning and asking to be clothed with His life-giving words. As I've said many times, "Apart from Him we can do nothing."

If we desire to reflect the radiance of Christ to the world, then we must allow God to change our words into ones that glorify Him and build up others. The Bible gives us a clear picture of life-giving words in Ephesians 4, which just so happens to be the apostle Paul's great teaching about taking off the old sinful nature and putting on the nature of Christ.

> You were taught, with regard to your former way of life, to **put off your old self**, which is being corrupted by its deceitful desires; to be made new in the attitude of your minds; and **to put on the new self**, created to be like God in true righteousness and holiness.
>
> Therefore each of you must **put off falsehood** and **speak truthfully** to his neighbor, for we are all members of one body. **"In your anger do not sin"**:

Do not let the sun go down while you are still angry, and do not give the devil a foothold. . . .

Do not let any unwholesome talk come out of your mouths, but only what is **helpful for building others up** according to their needs, that it may **benefit those who listen**. (Eph. 4:22–27, 29, emphasis added)

Choose to speak truth. The first thing we notice in this passage is the command to "put off falsehood" and to "speak truthfully" to one another. We all know lying is a sin, but I cannot move forward without addressing this issue because we live in a culture where lying is normalized and assumed. But, a radiant woman is one who knows she is "called out" of the darkness, and, for that reason, lying is not acceptable.

When I first surrendered my life to Jesus, I was a BIG liar. I have no qualms confessing this fact about the "old me" because this was one of the areas that Christ radically transformed in me immediately. I'm not that girl anymore. Back then I would lie to cover up my mistakes, make myself appear better, or just to get my way. But when Jesus, who is called "the Way, *the Truth*, and the Life," came into my life, He quickly pointed out the sin of lying and called me to repent.[9] I did repent, but genuine life change required one more step: I had to recognize my motive. The Holy Spirit began to show me *why* I lied.

Lying was a covering I used to hide my shame. Imagine that a lie is like a cover-up that we use when we don't necessarily want to be seen in our swimsuit. That's how I used lying. Ashamed of my sinful actions, I would wrap a lie around my waist to cover it up. Or, I wrapped myself in lies about my identity, abilities, or experiences so that I could appear superior in the eyes of others. Such a masquerade of lies! The upkeep was exhausting, and the outcome was far from radiant.

In repentance I found forgiveness. I also found the perfect cover-up for my shame: grace. Grace slipped over my head and easily and beautifully covered me, like a perfectly draped silken garment. When I 'fessed up and owned my sin, God took me into His arms and covered me in His grace. He helped me to understand that I didn't need to lie anymore because my sin was forgiven. I didn't need to try to hide behind a false identity because Jesus loves me exactly as I am. When we truly "get" what it means to be fully accepted in Christ, we don't have anything to prove or an image to maintain.

I would challenge any woman reading this to ask the Holy Spirit to open her eyes to see if or when she is speaking words of falsehood. Oftentimes we can get into bad sinful patterns and be unaware of it. Just ask Jesus; He will show you. Trust me; this is one area in which you definitely want freedom.

God is so good! Once He showed me my sin and revealed to me why I was lying, He healed my shame. By His grace, I am now free from wearing that old dirty cloak. I have put off falsehood and put on truth. This outfit is far more flattering and doesn't require the exhausting upkeep.

Choose words that build others up. "Wow, she was pretty until she opened her mouth" is not a statement that should be made about a radiant woman. I've heard this slam stated about gorgeous women whose looks turned sour when they began to speak. Friends, I don't want to be that girl! As I've confessed, my mouth has gotten me into trouble in the past, but I'm asking the Lord to help me speak words of truth and life every day. Transformation begins by seeing the power of our words.

We've all been in the presence of someone who can tear us down in an instant, and we've also been in the presence of a person who is so encouraging and life giving that their words cause us to feel built up.

Remember, "Do not let any unwholesome talk come out of your mouths, but only what is **helpful for building others up** according to their needs, that it may **benefit those who listen**" (Eph. 4:29, emphasis added). This verse instructs us to speak words that "build up" and "benefit" those who listen. The word picture here contrasts two construction crews: one who recklessly demolishes, tearing down a building with a wrecking ball; the other, who builds something up, using tools and supplies to carefully construct something beautiful. A radiant woman must choose which team she will work for—will her words tear people down or build people up? I hope all of us desire the same thing: to encourage and bless people with our words— thankfully God instructs us how to do it.

So, how do we build? Long ago I heard three simple questions that we should ask before speaking:

1. Are my words true?

2. Are my words necessary?

3. Are my words beneficial?

These questions provide the speaker with an easy way to evaluate whether or not they should say what is on the tip of their tongue.

Let's imagine I have something I want to tell a friend. So, I ask myself, "Is it true?" If the answer is yes, then I move on to the next question: "Is it necessary?" I hesitate. Sure, I could rationalize a reason my girlfriend should know the piece of information, but is it really necessary? Let's say I determine it is necessary for her to know, then that brings me to the last question: "Is it beneficial?" No, it would not benefit her or the person being discussed for me to share the information; therefore, I know that I should remain silent.

Over the years, when I've chosen to abide by this little three-step wonder, I've seen the benefit and blessing of restraint. I've had fewer and fewer moments of regret. As it says in Proverbs, "When words are many, sin is not absent" (10:19). The flip side of that coin is just as true: "When words are few, regret is absent."

Put on Humility

> Clothe yourselves with humility toward one another.
> (1 Pet. 5:5)

Recently, while scrolling through my favorite online news magazines, I stumbled upon an article about a Hollywood starlet who was overheard confessing her greatest fear. She was distressed that another actress, who was at that time battling cancer, would die, thereby ruining her chances of appearing on the cover of *People* magazine. Sadly her comment revealed her heart: she was more concerned with herself than she was with the potential death of another.

Before I sound critical or judgmental, let me be quick to confess that this same pride and selfishness is in me. Actually this selfishness is in every human being. The essence of sin is selfishness. Every one of us is born infected with the deadly virus. We want to be number one, to turn the proverbial spotlight on ourselves, and to do whatever it takes to have our own way. But a radiant woman is one who desires the spotlight turned away from her and onto the face of Jesus.

For that reason, radiance is radical!

When I was a little girl, my family lived in a house that was set upon a hill. Because I am one of seven siblings and my cousins lived nearby, there was always a throng of kids outside playing. We were a very imaginative troop! Of course, we played Hide and Seek, Red Rover, and I Spy, but a favorite of the group was a game called King of the Mountain. The goal was simple: each person would battle, maneuver, and scuffle to gain the position at the top of the hill, thereby naming herself "QUEEN OF THE MOUNTAIN!"

This is the essence of pride as well as the ultimate goal of the world from which Christ redeemed us. Our culture screams at us to make ourselves supreme, to live for our own interests, to do whatever it takes to seek our own happiness. This worldly mind-set produces only misery. Whenever we look out for our own interests at the expense of others, we are never ever satisfied, and in doing so we alienate anyone who would dare stand in the way.

It makes perfect sense then that a woman who chooses to "clothe herself in humility" seems a radical departure from the world, and gives evidence that a major transformation has occurred in her heart. No longer captive to the darkness of this world that bids her to seek self first, she is a citizen of God's kingdom, where humility is both a virtue and her lifestyle because she knows that God is the only King of the mountain. He is the one worthy of praise, honor, and adoration—not self.

Humility is the mark of a girl who sees God clearly and who, in turn, sees herself rightly—as a created being designed to glorify her Creator. The opposite of humility is pride, a conceited love of self. The Bible teaches us to, "Clothe [ourselves] with humility . . . because 'God opposes the proud but gives grace to the humble'" (1 Pet. 5:5). Why is humility required for radiance? Because humility is the act of glorifying God by choosing to place Him first, others second, and ourselves last. You see, pride demands center stage. Pride demands the attention and praise to be turned on self.

Pride doesn't care about the glory of God.

Pride will fight to have its way.

Pride will hurt others to feel superior.

Pride will ignore its own sin in order to point the finger at another's flaws.

Humility proves to be the perfect attire for the radiant woman because this attitude is the same as Christ Jesus. Philippians teaches us to "do nothing from selfishness or empty conceit, but with humility of mind regard one another as more important than yourselves; do not merely look out for your own personal interests, but also for the interests of others" (Phil. 2:3–4 NASB).

How do we "clothe ourselves in humility"? First, we must begin with God. Put God in His proper place in our hearts, and humility will naturally begin to flow. I heard Louie Giglio once say, "Humility is the instant right sizing of me that occurs with just one eyeful of His majesty." If we desire radiance, turn our eyes on Jesus: the Creator; the Sustainer; the All-Knowing, All-Powerful, Majestic, Holy, Sovereign Savior of the World. When we think rightly of Him, all of a sudden we don't think so much of ourselves. We do this by reading His Word and humbling ourselves in prayer—acknowledging our dependence and need for Him.

Before someone mistakenly assumes that humility then means low self-esteem, let me quickly say, "No." Humility, as C. S. Lewis said, "is not thinking less of yourself, it is thinking of yourself less."[10] I hope you can discern the difference. When God is in His rightful place in our hearts, then we see ourselves rightly: sinners in need of grace who are redeemed by the precious blood of Jesus. We recognize our true value and worth in Him, but at the same time, this truth humbles us.

Realizing our proper place is for our good, and we are blessed by it. For when we choose humility, we receive a surprising bonus: joy! The most miserable people in the world are those who center their lives upon self. Just think about the fights and disputes that come from wounded pride. Pride breeds unhappiness. It's easy to see why. At the core of our being we know we are only created beings; to think otherwise is to deny our humanity. When we attempt to ignore God and place ourselves at the center of the universe, we attempt the impossible. Placing ourselves (instead of our Creator) at the center proves a constant struggle and battle for importance, for supremacy, and for a sense of control that we truly can never attain.

When a radiant woman chooses to wear humility, she chooses to wear the garment in her closet that fits the best and therefore is the most flattering. Gone is the girl who would fight to be queen of the mountain because she knows the King of the mountain, and her chief desire is for others to see His light in her.

Listen to Your Stylist

Every episode of *What Not to Wear* hinges on a pivotal moment: will the fashion pupil listen to the advice and guidance of her stylists, or will she continue to dress in the manner that she did before? At some point in each episode, there is an opportunity for the pupil to shop alone. The poor lass is thrown into the shopping Mecca—New York City—alone but armed with an obnoxious amount of money and the words of her stylists as her guide.

Off she goes.

It usually only takes a few minutes before the shopper is drawn back to the very garments that her stylists threw away. Try as she may to stick to the rules, she is fondling a pair of "pleather" pants as if her entire happiness depends upon them.

While I've laughed at the silliness, I realize how very similar this scene is to my own life. Jesus rescued me from darkness and calls me to throw out the old clothes that represent that life: selfishness, drunkenness, promiscuity, greed, lust, and anger. Yet, there are days when I find myself going back to the garbage bin for one of these outfits.

In moments like these, we must choose to listen to our Stylist. Unlike the show, *What Not to Wear,* God doesn't send us out alone. He goes with us every step of the way. And so, in our moments of weakness when we are tempted to dress ourselves in pride, He gently reminds us of what His style manual, the Bible, says and He encourages us to choose humility instead. Or, when tempted to wear jealousy to a friend's wedding, the Holy Spirit will whisper, *Now jealousy is really not the best color for your complexion; why don't you wear "love" instead?*

After all, Love is the "little black dress" of the spiritual life.

SHINE ON!
Choose each day to clothe yourself with the radiance of Jesus Christ and take off the deeds of darkness.

For the eyes of the LORD *range throughout the earth to strengthen those whose hearts are fully committed to him.*

2 Chronicles 16:9

CHAPTER SIX

A Radiant Woman Has an Undivided Heart

A Divided Heart

Just twenty-two and new in town, I landed my first job after college working in public relations and was trying to scrape by on my entry-level income when I fell hard for a guy. In the midst of settling into my new apartment, new job, new city, and new social scene, I met my "dream man." Girls, when I tell you that he was everything I thought I ever wanted, on paper, I'm not kidding. Of course, I'm referring to the "future husband" list.

Where was I? Oh yes, smitten kitten.

So I met my Mr. Dreamy, and we started dating. He was handsome, charming, tall (like, I-could-wear-my-4-inch heels tall), smart, athletic, funny, and successful. As I said, "the list." We dated for a while, and the relationship got more serious. I was gaga over this guy, and it seemed that the feeling was mutual. We spent tons of time together, going to movies, great restaurants, concerts—the guy knew how to treat a girl. We had a blast exploring the city because we were both new in town.

Then, after a little while, I noticed that he grew distant and less enthusiastic about our dates. I couldn't quite put my finger on the problem at first. Although he was still asking me out when he wasn't out of town on business, he just seemed different. My girl radar was going off, but I eventually just chalked the cooling off to the inevitable ebb and flow of a dating relationship. Still, that distant feeling increased, and soon I felt like he was less interested in me. Trust me, that is not a fun feeling.

So one day I just asked him, "What's going on?" He tried to blow it off and said, "Nothing. I'm just busy at work, . . . blah, blah, blah." But I could tell it was more than that. So, after asking him to be honest, he finally looked at me and said, "Well, the truth is I haven't been going out of town for work. I've actually been seeing my ex-girlfriend for a few weeks now. My heart is so divided. I'm torn, and I feel so guilty. I was hoping I could date both of you until I figured out which relationship I wanted long term, but I guess that isn't going to work, is it?"

> Calling All Emergency Vehicles:
> smitten kitten found mortally wounded and lying in
> ditch on side of the road.

Yep, I was crushed, but years later I can laugh at the whole situation and how very naïve I was back then. I share that humiliating story with you to demonstrate the consequences of a divided heart. When a woman's heart is divided, she cannot maintain passion, joy, faithfulness, and closeness with both parties; one will eventually win—or in my case, lose.

As we learned in chapter 1, the radiant Christian life is based on a love relationship with Jesus. We desire to live for His glory and follow Him because we love Him. That being the case, doesn't it make sense that maintaining passion for God's glory remains our top priority? This love is a battlefield; therefore, we must fight to ensure that our hearts aren't divided and that we don't lose our fire for Jesus.

King David expressed his understanding of how easily our hearts can be lured away from God, in this prayer:

> Among the gods there is none like you, O Lord; no deeds can compare with yours. All the nations you have made will come and worship before you, O Lord; they will bring glory to your name. For you are great and do marvelous deeds; you alone are God. Teach me your way, O LORD, and I will walk in your truth; **give me an undivided heart**, that I may fear your name. (Ps. 86:8–11, emphasis added)

One thing I've discovered is this: if my life is to reflect Christ to the world, then my heart must be fully devoted to Him. Like King David, I've learned to ask God for an undivided heart.

The word *undivided* means complete, whole, unbroken, or fully united. When I pray for an undivided heart, I'm asking God to give me a heart that is fully united with His own.

Maintaining an undivided heart requires that we guard against the lures and enticements of our "ex." Yes, girls, we, too, have an ex that we loved before Jesus; his name is "The World." Stick with me here . . . this is an important truth that every radiant woman must know.

No Flirting with the Ex

First of all, our ex is the world system that Jesus Christ redeemed us from when we placed our faith in Him. James Boice describes the world as "an organized system, made up of a set of ideas, people, activities, purposes, used by Satan for opposing the work of Christ on earth. It is the very opposite of what is godly."[11] It is that very kingdom of darkness Boice describes that held us captive before Jesus rescued us, bringing us into the "kingdom of light" (Col. 1:12–13).

Let me explain some terminology that is basic to our understanding the battle for our hearts. Also, notice that I am no longer talking about a battle *of* the heart. I am now talking about a battle *for* our heart. When I say "the world," I'm not referring to the created order (nature) but to a world system that is opposed to and separated from God. This world system is ruled by Satan and is characterized by love of self above all else.

Jesus taught that we cannot avoid living in this world, but

that we, His followers, are not of this world any longer (John 17:16). Before Jesus Christ redeemed us, we all lived by the standards and practices of this world. As it says in Ephesians 5:8, we "were once darkness, but now [we] are light in the Lord." Although we are still surrounded by forces and influences opposed to God (darkness) and His ways, that's not who we are anymore . . . we are now light.

So, what is our ex like? In 1 John 2:15–17, we find a great description of our ex:

> Don't love the world's ways. Don't love the world's goods. Love of the world squeezes out love for the Father. Practically everything that goes on in the world—wanting your own way, wanting everything for yourself, wanting to appear important—has nothing to do with the Father. It just isolates you from him. The world and all its wanting, wanting, wanting is on the way out—but whoever does what God wants is set for eternity. (*The Message*)

Wow! John does not make our ex, the world, sound too attractive, does he? And while that may repel us on paper, does it in our daily lives? Think about it, and be honest with yourself. Essentially, worldliness is a life centered on self, *wanting our own way, wanting everything for ourselves, wanting to appear important.* It's a "me-first" agenda. Worldliness desires "what I want, when I want it" at the expense of anyone else. It desires things to make ourselves look better: Attention. Accolades. Possessions.

Worldliness desires one thing: its own glory. Truth be told, in the moment, when our guards are down and we are not feeling strong, don't we all consider a rebound with our ex?

This tainted desire leads to a serious problem: a divided heart. Simply stated, we cannot desire God's glory and our own glory at the same time. When we buy into the world's messages that scream, "It's all about me," then our hearts are turned away from loving Jesus. **Every woman must ask herself, "Am I influencing the world, or is the world influencing me?"** Remember, we are called to be light in the darkness, but so often we are naïve to the fact that the darkness is working hard and around the clock to put our lights out.

A great illustration of this truth is found in the biblical story of Samson and Delilah. Truly, theirs is one of the most soap-opera-esque stories in all of Scripture. If you haven't read it, I recommend flipping your Bible to the book of Judges, chapters 13–16 and reading Samson's story from start to finish. His life portrays the ramifications of a divided heart.

Samson was born to a God-fearing family in the midst of a seriously dark time in Israel's history. The nation had turned away from God and was living decadently without regard for the Lord's ways. (Sound a little familiar?) Yet, in the midst of this darkness, one family loved and feared the Lord. The Angel of the Lord appeared to a barren woman telling her that she would soon have a son and her child would be set apart to the Lord. The woman gave birth to a boy and named him Samson. He grew, and the Lord blessed him.

Samson was set apart to the Lord. Much like our calling as radiant women, we, too, are called out and set apart to display the glory of God in a godless world. Here's the coolest thing about the story—are you ready for this?—Samson's name meant *of the Light*. Samson as the lone man of God in his generation was the light bearer—the one whom all the others in darkness were to watch to know the way.

So, guess what happened? The enemies of God did everything and anything to thwart Samson's purpose and mission. Most of their attempts failed, except for one. Samson was lured and enticed away from God through a divided heart.

And Samson's lure had a name . . . Delilah.

Delilah was beautiful.

Delilah was seductive.

Delilah was the object of Samson's desire.

Over time, Delilah captured Samson's heart, and he disclosed to her the secret to his power: his devotion to the Lord. By the way, guess what Miss Delilah's name means: *of the Darkness*.

The entire story of Samson and Delilah symbolizes how darkness seduces, entices, and lures us into turning away from God. Samson (of the light) fell for the tricks of Delilah (of the darkness), and his divided heart led him to forsake his God-given role. Delilah was successful. Her charms overpowered Samson's commitment to the Lord, and he forsook his call to live as light.

Here are a few warning signs that our hearts are divided:

1. Our passion for God and His kingdom purposes begins to cool.
2. We become complacent about sin and lack conviction when we do rebel.
3. Our light in this dark world begins to diminish.

So, as you can see, a divided heart is a serious matter. Next, I will address the three arenas in which women battle worldliness: media, materialism, and entitlement.

Media

I use the term *media* broadly to describe the various mediums that provide us with information and entertainment: television, movies, Internet, magazines, social networking sites, and music. While I am a user and enjoyer of all of the above, I do recognize the need for discernment and discretion when it comes to what I watch and what I allow to influence my life. Hold your horses . . . I'm not pulling a *Footloose* and calling for a book burning or ban on TV. What I am cautioning is that we must be wise and discerning women, who guard ourselves against the world's deceptive lures designed to draw us away from Jesus.

Here are a few examples from my own life:

A few years ago, I noticed how **fashion magazines** caused my heart to drift from Jesus because I was fixated upon improving *my* image instead of exalting His. As I would flip through the pages of *Vogue, In Style, Elle, Shape,* and *Glamour,* I found myself dissatisfied with my body, my hair, and my wardrobe. This growing dissatisfaction with self and obsession with achieving the perfect look resulted in a life focused on attaining an impossible image. Sounds pretty much like the definition of worldliness, doesn't it? Think about it, where was my focus and attention during those years? On *me* and my ever-growing list of needed self-improvements. This state of frustration and lack of contentment are exactly what the advertisers hope will occur. They only sell their products if consumers are dissatisfied with their lives.

These joy stealers are everywhere: at the nail salon, in a doctor's waiting room, in the grocery store line, and in my mailbox. I was constantly bombarded with the message that I interpreted as, "Marian, you are not enough." And I ended up like a hamster on a wheel, running, spinning toward an unattainable finish.

I must repeat myself . . . I am not saying that reading fashion magazines is sinful. I am saying we need to use caution and be extremely wise concerning the degree to which our thinking and behavior are shaped by the images we see in the pages. One thing that helped me come back to a place of contentment and to refocus my life on Jesus was to stop buying the magazines and to cancel all store catalogs that enticed me to buy their products. I realize this may sound drastic, but I found such freedom in this decision. After a few months, feelings of contentment returned because I was no longer living under the pressure of the advertising industry, and my bank account was extremely grateful. Not only did I experience fewer battles with a negative self-image, but I also received the beautiful bonus of having more time to spend with God because I spent less time fixated on myself.

Now I must turn my attention to the usual suspects, the ones that are always mentioned in a conversation of this nature—the big daddies of them all: **television and movies**. I've definitely seen over the years how certain TV shows and movies can desensitize me toward sin and evil—the very sin that breaks the heart of God. Just think about it, programs that would have caused shock and awe ten years ago are commonplace today. Each year, our appetite and tolerance level increases, and the more we are exposed to images and messages of worldliness, the more we grow accustomed to the lifestyle. Over time we are programmed to think the lifestyle and behaviors we watch are not only normal but also desirable.

Satan, whose chief desire is to turn our hearts away from God, rules the world system in which we live. He's no fool; he knows the pathway to our hearts is through our minds; therefore, he cleverly uses the most attractive and alluring means to entice us away from God. The world's agenda finds a megaphone into our homes through television. I recently learned that the average middle school girl is exposed to roughly 280 sexual images a day. Images that reinforce with every frame that her value and worth as a woman are found in being used as a sexual object. Is it any wonder that an entire generation of young girls see themselves as usable goods? Is it shocking that we have young women who feel ashamed of their virginity? This is the result of the brainwashing that young girls endure on a daily basis. Radiant women . . . beware! We are not immune to deception. We are also inundated by these lies and messages on a daily basis.

Girlfriends, please say with me:

"I WILL NOT BE BRAINWASHED!"

I recently got to thinking about Hollywood's powerful impact on a woman's self-image. As a little girl, I vividly recall going to the theater with my sister to watch the movie *Grease.* Branded upon my mind was Sandy's transformation from a good, clean, wholesome girl to the black leatherclad, wild Pink Lady. The message was loud and clear: cool and fun is defined as wild and promiscuous, and purity and wholesomeness are characteristics of only the unlikable prissy and uptight girls. *Really?* Can a girl who is pure not be fun? She should be the most carefree, abandoned girl at the party because she knows that her radiance comes from the only true power Source. She doesn't have to undergo a leather makeover to be loved.

As I grew older, '80s movies became slumber party staples. We watched with abandon these coming of age movies: *Sixteen Candles, Pretty in Pink, The Breakfast Club,* and *Say Anything.* These movies taught us young girls to view purity as something shameful and to think maturity meant sexual experience. Looking back, I recognize how my movie choices played a significant role in shaping the woman I became in my young adulthood. I was fed a steady diet of the world's message, and my lifestyle definitely evidenced this fact. Today I've wised up to media's powerful influence in my life, and I make choices accordingly.

Because I love God and I want to live for His glory, I've decided to limit the quantity of time I spend watching TV and choose wisely which programs and movies that I do watch. The old saying goes, "Garbage in, garbage out." **Overtime, even the best defenses are worn down if repeatedly attacked.** If I allow myself to be exposed to and entertained by something that encourages sinful and ungodly behavior, then eventually my heart will grow cold toward God and my life could begin to mirror what I see. C. J. Mahaney in his excellent book *Worldliness* explains how easily media can influence us:

> Just because we don't instantly mimic all we see doesn't mean our hearts aren't negatively affected by the programs or films we watch. Tugging like a subtle undertow below the surface, the media can tempt us to drift toward the world.
>
> Drift toward worldliness may be slow, its symptoms not immediately apparent. This drift is usually a sign of dulling conscience. The conscience doesn't function like a light switch—one moment the lights are on, then everything is dark with a flip of the switch. Instead, the sensitivity of our conscience is dulled over time as it is resisted or ignored.[12]

As many of you know, I was at one time a fan of *The Bachelor* reality TV show, but that all changed this past season. I was watching one night with my girlfriends, when I just felt sick to my stomach about the way the program depicted love and marriage. I realized that God was not glorified by the content on the show, and my heart was doused by messages that are opposed to God's ways. Messages such as "If it feels good, do it." Or my personal favorite, "Just follow your heart." These clichés are thrown about as excuses for cheating, lying, and outright selfish behavior.

I don't have the space to write why this is such a horrible philosophy by which to live. I'll just briefly say that our feelings are fickle and can't be trusted as reliable guides; we must make decisions based upon truth and pray for a conscience that is led by true conviction. Otherwise, we are people led by every whim and impulse. Seriously girls, does anyone really want a guy who falls in and out of "love" within hours. That is just not someone we would trust in the context of marriage—scratch that; we wouldn't trust him through dinner.

If I hear another guy (or girl) say she loves someone one hour and then supposedly fell out of love with the same person the next hour, I might implode. This abuse of the word *love* is detrimental to women and our culture as a whole. We now have an entire generation who believes love is a feeling that lasts only until the next commercial break. Satan has cleverly brainwashed us into thinking a relationship is only meant to last as long as it feels good. Frankly, I would much rather these people call it what it is, "hooking up," because that is all that they are doing—they are not in love.

This is just one example of how the world influences our thinking and, therefore, our behavior. We must guard ourselves against pressures that will persuade us to live in such a way that doesn't honor God. So, after seeing *The Bachelor's* negative influence on women, I knew that watching this program was no longer an option for me. I didn't make this choice in a legalistic manner. No, I decided to break up with *The Bachelor* because I love God and want Jesus glorified in my life. I realized that, *for me*, watching a show that glorifies godless behavior was not only a waste of an hour on Monday nights, but it also may appear to the room full of friends who watched the show with me that I condoned the very behavior that I write books and give talks to discourage—the very behavior that dims radiance and grieves the heart of the Radiant One.

Before you fling your flat-screen (or this book), just ask God what He would have you to watch or not to watch. One of my favorite aspects of the Christian life is the freedom we have in Christ—freedom from legalistic rules and regulations. God placed His Holy Spirit in our hearts so that He can lead us in every moment of decision. With the Spirit's help, every woman can choose what programs are best for her.

> Please don't misunderstand. I'm not saying it's wrong to watch television, rent a DVD, surf the Internet, or spend an evening at the cinema. The

hazard is thoughtless watching. **Glorifying God is an intentional pursuit.** We don't accidently drift into holiness; rather, we mature gradually and purposefully, one choice at a time. In the Christian walk, we can't just step on the right path and figure all is well. Christian discipleship is a lifelong journey consisting of a series of countless steps. Each step matters, and thus our viewing habits matter.

—C. J. Mahaney[13]

Trust me; I absolutely love movie night with my girlfriends more than anything. Popcorn and peanut M&Ms are the best! So I've found the following question to be helpful in making these decisions about what to watch: *Does this show encourage me to glorify God, or does it glorify ungodliness and pull my heart away from Him?* As I've asked this question, I've found that sometimes I'm led to watch a movie or program that I normally would not have and discovered in it the beautiful story of redemption (for example, the movie *Taken*). Other times, I choose to turn off something that is blatant propaganda for a godless lifestyle. Every time, the deciding factor is my love for Jesus. I don't want to pollute my mind with anything that would draw my heart away from Him.

Materialism

Media is just one method the world uses to entice us away from God; materialism is another. Materialism is a focus on and a trust in what we can touch and possess. Or materialism can be defined as finding contentment or identity in the purchase and possession of material goods. It describes "the unchecked desire for, dependence on, and stockpiling of stuff."[14] When possessing goods is exalted to a godlike status, we fall prey to the notion that we must have something in order to feel happy. Then we become captive to the clutches of a materialistic world. As a result of this captivity (the love of things), our hearts grow cold toward God.

The world's self-seeking agenda whispers in our ear that we cannot be content unless we acquire, own, or possess the latest or the greatest. I noticed how this materialistic mind-set crept into my life after buying my house. As I said earlier, I became obsessed with watching home decorating shows. A daily dose of decorating divas left me feeling dissatisfied with the home that only a few months earlier I had been thrilled with and felt I had been blessed with a home that exceeded my expectations.

This is how the home decorating shows sucked me in. As the latest gadgets and designs were paraded before me, I felt dissatisfied and thought the remedy would be new countertops, convection oven, crown molding, drawer pulls, hardwoods, silk drapes, thicker crown molding, monogrammed pillows, and definitely,

definitely a double-headed shower . . . even though I live alone. Get the picture?

So, as a result of the materialistic brainwashing, I found myself buying things that I did not need and spending all of my "free" time hunting for home items. Weeks into the process, not only did I feel drained both emotionally and financially; I realized I was missing something—my time with God. Without really noticing, my time had been sucked into this consuming vortex. My thoughts and energies were distracted away from Jesus but fully devoted to the pursuit of the "perfect living space." Of course, I felt drained because I was attempting to fill my life with stuff instead of filling my life with Jesus.

As we all know, the scenario I described above can be replicated using clothes, shoes, cars, or anything the human heart can desire and acquire. We can become obsessed with buying things and never become aware that we've fallen prey to the world's materialistic agenda. The problem arises when the desire for stuff squeezes out our love for Jesus and divides our devotion.

I finally got to the point where I was sickened by the covetousness of it all. God revealed to me how those shows enticed greed in me. As a result, I would spend money on things I did not need. Once I wised up to what was going on, I stopped watching those home shows and stopped wasting my time and my money. The result? Peace, joy, and contentment returned, and I discovered more time to spend with Jesus.

Coveting is desiring stuff too much or desiring too much stuff. It's replacing our delight in God with joy in stuff. Materialism is what happens when coveting has cash to spend . . . The sin of covetousness is not that we have stuff; it's that our stuff has us. . . . . Affluence can be a spiritual disability that dulls people to their need for God. —C. J. Mahaney[15]

Consequences of a Divided Heart

Remember the story about the smitten kitten? The smitten kitten (aka *me*) was the unfortunate recipient of a divided heart. I went on to explain how the guy kept returning to his ex. We all do the same thing at times; we return to the world from which we were rescued. Well, when we do return to our ex, the world, what are our consequences? There are two: moral compromise and missed blessings. These consequences of a divided heart are played out in dramatic and historical record in Scripture in the story of King David's son, Solomon. Remember King David's prayer in Psalm 86:11 when he asked the Lord, "give me an undivided heart"? Apparently Solomon didn't get this memo. He was pulled away by another "lover" like so many others who began with a passionate love for God,

Solomon's relationship with the Lord began on a high note. He was determined to honor God, and he built a temple for His glory. God blessed him, granting him both unparalleled wisdom and extravagant wealth. However, the Lord warned King Solomon early on of the dangers of a divided heart:

> "As for you, if you walk before me in integrity of heart and uprightness, as David your father did, and do all I command and observe my decrees and laws, I will establish your royal throne over Israel forever, as I promised David your father when I said, 'You shall never fail to have a man on the throne of Israel.'
>
> "But if you or your sons turn away from me and do not observe the commands and decrees I have given you and go off to serve other gods and worship them, then I will cut off Israel from the land I have given them and will reject this temple I have consecrated for my Name. Israel will then become a byword and an object of ridicule among all peoples."
> (1 Kings 9:4–7)

God is clear. There are blessings for those of us whose hearts are faithful and fully devoted, but there are also consequences when our hearts are entangled and pulled away. As we see in Scripture, Solomon's heart, enticed by other lovers, turned away from God.

> King Solomon was obsessed with women. Pharaoh's daughter was only the first of the many foreign women he loved—Moabite, Ammonite, Edomite,

Sidonian, and Hittite. He took them from the sur-
rounding pagan nations of which GOD had clearly
warned Israel, "You must not marry them; they'll
seduce you into infatuations with their gods."
Solomon fell in love with them anyway, refusing to
give them up. He had seven hundred royal wives
and three hundred concubines—a thousand women
in all! And they did seduce him away from God. As
Solomon grew older, his wives beguiled him with
their alien gods and he became unfaithful—he
didn't stay true to his GOD as his father David had
done. Solomon took up with Ashtoreth, the whore
goddess of the Sidonians, and Molech, the horrible
god of the Ammonites. . . .

GOD was furious with Solomon for abandoning
the GOD of Israel, the God who had twice appeared
to him and had so clearly commanded him not to
fool around with other gods. Solomon faithlessly
disobeyed GOD's orders.

GOD said to Solomon, "Since this is the way
it is with you, that you have no intention of keeping faith with me and doing what I have commanded, I'm going to rip the kingdom from you
and hand it over to someone else. But out of respect
for your father David I won't do it in your lifetime. It's your son who will pay—I'll rip it right
out of his grasp. Even then I won't take it all; I'll

> leave him one tribe in honor of my servant David
> and out of respect for my chosen city Jerusalem."
> (1 Kings 11:1–5, 9–13 *The Message*)

I never fail to feel sadness when I read King Solomon's story. I also feel a sense of trepidation knowing how easily the human heart is prone to wander. Moral compromise and missed blessings do result from a heart that is divided. As I learned early in my Christian walk, my heart *will* follow whatever it loves the most.

A Word on Dating and Marriage

As I've ministered to college and single women over the years, I've seen time and time again the consequences of a divided heart unfold. Sadly I've watched as girls who love Jesus walk away from Him when their hearts were torn by the desires of the world, or when they squeezed out their loyalty to Jesus.

One major issue I must address before this chapter draws to a close is the issue of a radiant woman dating or marrying someone who does not profess Jesus Christ as Lord and Savior. Scripture is clear on this point. Christians are not to be unequally yoked with non-Christians (2 Cor. 6:14). The reason is simple: like King Solomon, if we love someone who does not love our God, then our hearts will be torn, our loyalty divided, and our commitment ultimately brought to the test. In marriage, the stakes are even higher when we consider the enormity of life decisions that a couple makes. If both parties aren't living for the glory of God and focused on loving Jesus, then their priorities will be at odds. For that reason, we who love God should not even put ourselves in a place of temptation to marry a non-Christian.

Recently I walked through this very issue with a friend of mine. She met a great guy with whom she shared so many common interests, and there was definitely the "click" factor. The only problem was that this guy was not a Christian. She dated him for a few months hoping that he would see Christ in her and desire what she had. But sadly, instead of him wanting her Jesus, what transpired was that her heart began to feel torn and soon she was put into a place of moral compromise because this young man did not share her values. Because his morals were based on the world's value systems, he continually pressured her to live in a way that did not honor God. My friend was a light who was dating a person living in the darkness.

Once she woke up and realized what was happening, her heart was already entangled. She'd fallen for this guy and had to make the tough choice of walking away from the relationship. She saw that he was pulling her away from Jesus, and now she understood why God calls Christians to marry other Christians. Because we marry whom we date, then it makes sense that we should refrain from dating anyone we wouldn't marry so that our hearts don't get entangled.

I must pause right here and say a word to any married women reading this book. Some of you may be married to nonbelievers.

If that is your situation, the Word of God is also clear about what you are to do: stay married! While the Bible commands those of us who are unmarried to wait and marry someone who is a committed follower of Jesus Christ, to the married women there is a different command. If someone is already married and her spouse is not a Christian, the Bible tells that woman to stay faithful, to shine brightly, and to pray fervently for God to change the heart of her spouse (1 Cor. 7:10–14).

My prayer is for both single and married women, for our hearts to stay fully devoted to the Lord. King Solomon is a warning to all of us. We are so easily enticed and drawn away from our pure devotion to Jesus. When this happens, we miss out on God's blessings, and our radiance is diminished if not completely snuffed out. I challenge you to pray with me the words of Psalm 86:11—"give me an undivided heart!"

Bind My Wandering Heart to Thee

> Come, thou Fount of every blessing,
> tune my heart to sing thy grace;
> streams of mercy, never ceasing,
> call for songs of loudest praise.

These are the opening lines to one of my all-time favorite hymns, "Come, Thou Fount of Every Blessing." The hymnist, Robert Robinson, was a guy wasting his life away in a drunken stupor until he and some of his drinking buddies went to heckle the famous evangelist George Whitefield. Instead of mocking, Robinson's life was forever changed by the message he heard that day. After surrendering his life to the Lord, he wrote his most famous hymn. One stanza of this much beloved hymn speaks powerfully to the issue of a divided heart.

> O to grace how great a debtor
> daily I'm constrained to be!
> Let thy goodness, like a fetter,
> bind my wandering heart to thee.
> Prone to wander, Lord, I feel it,
> prone to leave the God I love;
> here's my heart, O take and seal it,
> seal it for thy courts above.[16]

Robinson recognized the tendency in each of us to wander away from the God we love. Ironically, after writing these words he fell back into his old sinful lifestyle. His heart, enticed by the lures of the world, turned away from the Lord. But, as his hymn so beautifully describes, God's grace extends to us even when we wander from Him.

One day while on a stagecoach traveling through England, a young woman offered an unhappy and dejected-looking stranger a word of encouragement by reading a hymn to him. The stranger was Robert Robinson, and the hymn she chose was the very one that he had penned many years before, "Come, Thou Fount of Every Blessing." As the young woman read the words, God's grace wooed him back.[17]

Perhaps you are like Robert Robinson and have drifted away from God. For whatever reason, the love you once felt has grown cold. Friends, let me encourage you with this reminder: God's goodness *is* a fetter that binds our wandering hearts to Him. This means, plainly and simply, He will never let us go. We belong to Him. That is the beauty of God's grace—because we never earned it, we can never lose it.

As I reflect back over my life, the one thing that I'm certain of is this: God has never let go of me. Even when I've blown it big time, He is still the God who covers my sin with His grace. Understanding the depth of His mercy causes my heart to love Him more.

If you've been enticed by the world or made some foolish choices, let the "streams of mercy" that Robinson so passionately praised draw your heart back home. God loves us, and He wants each of us to break it off once and for all with our ex because He desires so much better for us. Friends, it is never too late . . . it never is with Jesus.

> *Here's my heart, Lord,*
> *take and seal it,*
> *seal it for thy courts above.*

SHINE ON!

A radiant woman should ask herself often, "Am I influencing the world or is the world influencing me?"

Since, then, you have been raised with Christ, set your hearts on things above, where Christ is seated at the right hand of God. Set your minds on things above, not on earthly things.

Colossians 3:1–2

CHAPTER SEVEN

A Radiant Woman Leaves
a Legacy

Let Your Light Shine Bright

W*ebster's* dictionary defines the word *legacy* as, "A thing handed down by a predecessor." It is something transferred from one generation to the next. I spent a recent evening honoring a woman whose life truly left a lasting legacy—countless people were influenced for eternity because of her choice to follow Jesus and make Him known. The woman was my friend Jill Jarvis Attebery.

Try as I may to comb through the mental scrapbook of my formative years, I can't remember first meeting Jill. I've always known her. My earliest memories include her. Snapshots of my childhood flash before me—Sunday school; first, second, and third grade to twelfth grade; slumber parties; school plays; choir trips; youth lock-ins, and drill team. Even with all these memories, I never imagined I would be asked to speak in memory of my earliest friend.

I was in Manhattan when the news reached me. My Blackberry began beeping wildly, first with text messages, then e-mails, and finally Facebook. All reported the same news. My friend Jill had tragically died in a car accident. This was one of those "I'll never forget where I was when I heard" moments. Standing near a subway line in Brooklyn, trying desperately to hear over the noise of the crowded streets and grappling with the reality of what I'd just learned. Stunned. Numb. Silent. The experience was a stark contrast to the bustling street whirling about me.

It was hours later, while walking through the fall foliage in Central Park with one of my best friends, that I began to process Jill's death. Still today, it doesn't seem real. As I walked through the park observing the change of seasons, I shared my memories of Jill from the season of girlhood.

I always thought she was perfect. She was the girl to whom I always came in second. Her gifts were numerous. She was good at everything. I recalled her beautiful singing voice, incredible leadership abilities, and her wisdom and intelligence. Jill was not one to waste her gifts . . . she used them all to the glory of God. Out of all the girls I knew growing up, I would describe Jill as the most radiant. She simply glowed. Her life was one that brought the light of Christ to others. Without a doubt, everyone who knew Jill knew that she loved Jesus. She wasn't shy about that fact.

For instance, when we were in eighth grade, a group of girls got together for a slumber party. Mix twenty-five middle school girls in one room and you definitely have the makings for drama. And boy, did we ever have drama! One of the girls decided it would be a great idea if we "played a game." Recalling the evening, I would describe it more as torture than a game, but that's beside the point. So the game was as follows: one by one, each girl left the room and while she was out, the other girls discussed everything about her and decided the five things they didn't like.

I'm sure you know where this game was headed . . . Dramaville.

So, one at a time, desperate for acceptance and too afraid to stand up to the Queen Bee, each girl left the room and awaited her critique: "You need to get braces." "You need to lose weight." "You need to . . ."

The game only lasted a few rounds until it was a blood bath. Tears everywhere. Girls fighting. Enough was enough. In the midst of all this girl drama, Jill stood up and said, "I can't play this game. I want you all to know something. You may not like everything about me, but what I hope you know is that I love Jesus and I want my life to glorify Him."

Like a lit candle when electricity goes out, so was Jill's decision in that moment to stand for Jesus. Darkness dispelled.

Light beamed. Glory. I'll never forget the impact her radiance had on me. For the first time, I witnessed the connection between loving God and living for God. Her love for Him extended far beyond a momentary pledge. She genuinely loved and cared for others; she passionately pursued God's purposes; and she produced the fruit such as kindness, goodness, gentleness, and patience—Jill's light shined brightly for Jesus.

A Lasting Legacy

Jill and I reunited months before her death because of our shared passion for reaching women with the gospel of Jesus Christ. I was devastated when the tragic news of her death reached me. Because I was in New York, I was unable to attend her funeral and share, alongside many others, the tremendous example Jill had been in my life. I later asked God for an opportunity to honor my friend and to testify to how much she had influenced my walk with Jesus.

A few weeks ago her husband e-mailed me, expressing his desire to honor Jill's dedication to God and to celebrate her legacy of discipleship through a women's event at his church. He asked if I would speak to the women that she'd touched. I jumped at the opportunity. I, too, had been impacted by her faithfulness.

It is not often that one has the privilege of surveying the legacy of someone's life. I already knew that Jill's life had impacted many people. When the news of her death was publicized, a flood of testimonies declaring her life's influence poured forth. Still, I was not prepared for the number of women who would drive from states away to honor the woman who'd played such a wonderful role in their lives.

The celebration was filled with women, young and old, who knew and loved Jill. Many she had discipled and had challenged them to memorize entire books of the Bible. Others she had taught in Sunday school. All of the women were impacted as she led praise and worship. They shared common gratitude for a friend who took time to listen and pray. Many others testified of her faithful encouragement during their shared struggle with infertility. One woman was extremely grateful for the steadfast support that Jill gave her when her daughter was killed years before. As she put it, Jill "walked through the valley of the shadow of death with me." We all missed a woman who had manifested the love of Christ through tangible expressions of His heart—depositing goodness, kindness, healing, hope, and faith in the lives of the women she encountered.

If a legacy is a "thing handed down," then Jill's life perfectly embodied the meaning of the word. Because of her life, hundreds of women came to know Jesus and devoted their lives to His kingdom. Her life sparked a love for His glory in others and spread far beyond her own circle of influence. Jill's legacy continues to grow. My friend Gina came with me to the celebration to lead worship. Although Gina did not personally know Jill, she walked away from the event challenged to follow her example.

Although I didn't know Jill, I have been impacted
by hearing of her life in Christ. Seeing the fruit of
her life deeply touched me, and I left her celebration
challenged to live for God's glory and to love others more deeply and intentionally as Jesus did—as
Jill, His servant did. I don't know who exactly said
or spoke this, but in my words, "Never underesti-
mate the power of one." The power of one life fully
devoted to knowing Jesus and making Him known.
This kind of RADICAL love can literally change
lives, families, towns, cities and nations. The power
of ONE—that will stick with me forever.

I love that expression, "the power of one." Jill's legacy is
certainly a powerful one. She proved that *one* life could leave
an impact for eternity—if focused on Christ and lived for His
glory. As Gina said, Jill's legacy has challenged me. It has challenged me not to waste one single day, not to lose perspective
about the purpose of this life, and not to get distracted from
what really matters. I know without doubt that Jill has heard
Jesus say, "Well done, my good and faithful servant." I pray we
will all be inspired and live in a manner that will bring us to
hear the same.

As I stood in that room, surrounded by the legacy of my
friend Jill, I sensed the Lord speak to me: *This is Radiance.*
Radiant women understand the "power of one" and live their
lives in such a way that we will leave a lasting legacy.

As I reflected on the things that made Jill's life shine so brightly, God showed me from Scripture the three things we women must do in order to leave a legacy. We will examine these characteristics through the life of the apostle Paul, who, like Jill, left a legacy that continues to bear fruit. To leave a legacy, radiant women must live intentionally, must live for eternity, and must live to lead others to Jesus.

1. To Leave a Legacy We Must Live Intentionally

One thing I've realized is that a legacy doesn't just happen accidently. It's not as if we wake up one day and remark, "Wow! How did that happen? Look at this legacy I have!" No, that's not how it works. To leave a legacy, a woman must live *intentionally*.

Intentional means deliberate—to purposefully act and live in certain ways in order to produce a desired outcome. We all know how this works. If we desire to stay in shape, then we are intentional about exercising and disciplined about what we eat. If we desire a successful career, then we are intentional about producing excellent work and prioritizing our time in order to focus on the required tasks. The same is true of radiant women's legacies. We deliberately choose to live in such a way that every day, every moment, every hour counts for Jesus.

The apostle Paul's life is one that is easily described as intentional. This means that Paul was determined, resolved, focused, and unswerving in his dedication to live a radiant life. In Texas, we have a saying "he was like a dog on a bone." I was reminded of this saying a few nights ago when my roommate's dog Sophie who happens to love sleeping in my bedroom, was rewarded with a bone. Usually Sophie is quite ladylike and minds her manners, curling up quietly at the foot of my bed. Yet, she's not so docile when a bone is involved. A determined and unswerving passion rose up in the little pooch to acquire every last drop of marrow, and she was undeterred in her mission. No amount of my scolding or pleading for peace and quiet would keep her away from the object of her delight. Sophie, like the apostle Paul, was intentional.

Girls, I want you to hear Paul's passion and to see what intentional living looks like in the following passage. Take note of his unwavering determination, his life focus, and his intentionality.

> I gave up all that inferior stuff so I could **know Christ personally**, experience his resurrection power, be a partner in his suffering, and go all the way with him to death itself. If there was any way to get in on the resurrection from the dead, I wanted to do it.
>
> I'm not saying that I have this all together, that I have it made. But I am well on my way, **reaching out for Christ**, who has so wondrously reached out for me. Friends, don't get me wrong: By no means

do I count myself an expert in all of this, but **I've got my eye on the goal**, where God is beckoning us onward—to Jesus. I'm off and running, and I'm not turning back.

So **let's keep focused on that goal,** those of us who want everything God has for us. If any of you have something else in mind, something less than total commitment, God will clear your blurred vision—you'll see it yet! Now that we're on the right track, let's stay on it. (Phil. 3:10–16 *The Message*, emphasis added)

Like I said, Paul was a "dog on a bone." He wasn't concerned with gaining popularity, achieving worldly success, or creating status or prestige. Only one thing mattered to him and that was to know Jesus Christ. The above passage reveals Paul's consuming pursuit of Jesus. He wanted to know Christ and to live for Christ. This passion is the first key to intentional living. If a radiant woman desires to leave a legacy, she must intentionally seek Jesus.

Intentionally Seek Jesus

My friend Jill clearly understood this principle. Her life was centered on pursuing Jesus. When I visited their home, her husband shared with me Jill's prayer journals. Sitting in the corner of a room stood a stack of binders, filled with years' and years' worth of time spent with Jesus. There were journals dating back to when she was just a little girl and even the one she used the day she died. Jill was intentional in her pursuit of a relationship with Jesus.

I opened one of the journals and flipped to a page where at the top I noticed her morning routine:

5am   seek the lord

       worship

       pray

       read the word

6am   exercise, get dressed, breakfast

7am   go to work

My first thought was, *Yikes! 5:00 a.m.* My second thought was, *That's intentional.* Before anything else, Jill would seek the Lord. To seek Him means we spend time with Him, worshipping, reading Scripture, and praying. Before you throw the book across the room and plan to hit the snooze button in the morning, I want to explain what I mean by *seek the Lord.* We all are created differently, with varying personalities and temperaments. So how one person seeks the Lord will look different from how another person does. Don't freak out if you and 5:00 a.m. don't get along so well.

The main thing is that our hearts are determined to engage with God in a personal way on a daily basis. Realizing that we can't live this life apart from Him, like the branch that desperately needs connection to the vine, we understand that we must connect to Christ if we are to radiate Him (John 15:1–5). The driving force is that we long for Him.

You know when you are in a relationship with a guy; you want to spend time with him. It's simple really. You can't wait to talk to him. You look forward all day long until you can finally see him and those cute little dimples of his. This is how a radiant woman pursues her relationship with Jesus. Her heart is intentionally set on spending time with Christ. Because, like the apostle Paul, she wants to know Him and to live for Him.

How this works out for each individual is, well . . . individual. Do not try to form a legalistic set of rules and then start striving hard to seek God. That attitude is missing the point. We pursue Him *because* we love Him, and time with the One we love is the greatest desire of our hearts. We are so in love with Jesus that we can't wait to meet with Him.

Here are a few pointers from my own devotional time that may help you intentionally seek the Lord:

- Spend time in prayer surrendering your life, your day, your activities, and your needs to the Lord. Ask for His power, provision, and protection. Some people roll out of bed, hit their knees, and pray before doing any other activity. I think this is wise. The act of bowing before God in prayer is an intentional posture that says, "You are God. Take my life. I give You everything. I need You." From that position of surrender, one can focus on Him.

Prayer is by no means limited to a specific position or place; it can occur on our knees, at a desk, driving to work, or sitting at the breakfast table. We can pray anywhere. Remember, God is always with us, and we are always in His presence. The key is to intentionally seek Him.

I recognize the fact that prayer is difficult for many of us. George MacDonald says, "Men and women were originally created to desire communion with God. But the effects of sin have dulled most of that original human desire. Sin turned a natural activity into an unnatural function."[18] Not only must we fight our own sin nature when it comes to prayer, but we also must fight against the world, which battles against our desire to commune with God. MacDonald addressed this problem:

> Few people realize how brainwashed each of us is. Messages bombard our private worlds (devotional and prayer time) every day, telling us that anything of a spiritual nature is a waste of time. From our earliest years we are subtly taught that the only way to achieve anything is through action. But prayer is a form of inaction . . . it does not seem to accomplish anything.[19]

MacDonald hit the nail on the head. There is an intense war against our prayer lives. Of course there is! Prayer moves mountains. Prayer connects us to the heart of God. Prayer gives us strength and power to face every situation. It only makes sense that our enemy dreads our spending one minute with God in prayer. I've faced this battle in my own prayer life. But since recognizing that it is a clash of wills, I've determined in my soul to press through the distractions and the noise to meet with God because I know *apart from Him I can do nothing.*[20]

- **Spend time reading and meditating upon God's Word.** Devotional Bible reading can occur in the morning or evening, or even during your lunch break. Whatever time of day works best for you is fine; I just can't stress enough how vital time reading God's Word is. We need it desperately. As Jesus said, "Man does not live on bread alone, but on every word that comes from the mouth of God" (Matt. 4:4).

In my personal quiet time, I use a daily Bible reading plan. Currently, I read a portion of the Old Testament, a portion of the New Testament, and a Psalm and a Proverb every day. I spend about thirty minutes every morning reading God's Word, and the payoff from this small investment is hugely significant in my life. As I read, I keep a journal and write down the insights and Scriptures that speak to me. This allows me to interact with God about His Word.

Often, I will pick a portion of Scripture and meditate on a specific verse. No, I'm not holding my Bible in one hand while doing a yoga pose. Meditation means to think, ponder, and mull over a specific truth until I *own it*. To reflect on it and study it until the truth is absorbed. George MacDonald writes, "The act of meditation is like tuning the spirit to heavenly frequencies. One takes a portion of Scripture and simply allows it to enter into the deepest recesses of self."[21]

As I proceed through my daily Bible reading, I listen to God. If the Holy Spirit causes me to pause on a certain verse, or if there is a truth that applies to a situation in my life, this is where I stop to meditate. My meditation process is *read the verse, write the verse, say the verse, and repeat*. Each time I do this I gain new insight and understanding, and the truth feeds my soul. Throughout my day, God brings to mind the truth and uses His Word as a guide in moments of decision or simply just to encourage me.

- **Spend time praising and worshipping God.** Worship is the chief activity of the human soul. We are worshippers; therefore, when we do what God created us to do, we are blessed. Worship brings peace, joy, and hope to our hearts because it sets our minds on who God is. Throughout our days, we should turn on praise music, sing out loud of His goodness, and tell God how great He is.

We are created for connection with our Creator. As a result, we function best when we prioritize our lives around seeking Him. Gary Thomas, in his incredible book *Holy Available,* reminds us that intentionally spending time with the Lord each day is crucial for our spiritual growth:

> Everywhere around us, we are reminded of what happens when we stop "tending." A garden can be overcome by weeds in a shockingly short period of time. If I don't change the oil in my car, the engine will break down. If I don't take a shower, I will start to stink. In the same way, a soul that isn't taken care of, a heart that isn't tended, won't support a healthy life. If we are not intentional about our spiritual growth, not only will we stop growing; we'll regress.[22]

When we intentionally seek Jesus, our lives are centered and focused instead of overwhelmed and empty. We now operate out of a heart that is surrendered to God's will and sensitive to His touch. As we carry on our daily activities, we are doing so connected to Christ and filled with His Spirit. This, my friends, is the start to a very radiant morning.

Intentionally Set Your Priorities

Do you ever feel like you are pulled in a million different directions? School, work, family, meetings, friends, ministry, exercise, shopping, paying bills. When I get the pulled feeling, I'm often frustrated and exhausted, which doesn't produce radiance. More often than not, I've found the problem is that I've allowed someone other than Jesus to set my priorities, and as a result my time has evaporated. George MacDonald wisely said, "Where your priorities are, there your time will be."[23]

The apostle Paul is a man who understood the call on his life, and as a result he set his priorities accordingly. Acts 26:17–18 describes Paul's life mission as given by Jesus: *"I am sending you, to open their eyes so that they may turn from darkness to light and from the dominion of Satan to God, in order that they may receive forgiveness of sins and an inheritance among those who have been sanctified by faith in Me"* (NASB). Paul clearly understood his mission and knew that he had key tasks to perform, and then he measured his use of his time against his mission. What was the result? Paul rocked the world with the glory of God!

Radiant women, it is time for us to rise up!!! We cannot fall into the cultural traps of apathy and laziness, or even the busyness that can take us away from prioritizing Christ. We cannot waste our lives, missing out on the high calling that God has for each one of us.

Yes, I'm talking to you. *You* are called of God. *You* have a part to play in His kingdom. *You* are extremely significant in God's purposes. If all of us don't wake up, seize the day, and align our lives with God's will, we will get to the end of our lives and have very little to show for it.

In case you feel like I'm being tough, I am! But before I preach to anyone else, I preach to myself. I have lived so long using A.D.D. as an excuse for procrastination and for missing out on all that God has for me. No more! I know a radiant woman is one who lives intentionally by setting her priorities according to her purpose *to reflect the radiance of Jesus*. And because the one pure and holy passion of my life is to glorify Him, then I must overcome any obstacles that stand in the way of that goal, even if that obstacle is myself.

Intentionally setting priorities will look different for each woman because we are all called, positioned, and gifted in different ways. Yet, how we steward this gift is a choice each of us must make. I have a small plaque in my room that reads, *Who we are, is God's gift to us. What we become, is our gift to God.*

One of the most helpful things we can do in our devotional time with God is to pray through and about our upcoming day. A helpful prayer to say is, "Jesus, please order my steps according to Your will." This simple prayer invites God to be God of our calendar and encourages us to evaluate the items on our agendas through His eyes. The goal of this prayer is to align our lives with our God-given purpose. Sometimes that means we will need to say no to certain activities and yes to others. We should always look to Jesus as our guide.

Can I be honest? This lesson I learned the hard way. I spent most of my life in a "reactionary" mode—simply *reacting* to the demands of the day and the cries of the urgent. I'm sure you can imagine how chaotic and stressful this would be. Sure, I was busy, but was I productive? My time seemed to disappear, and I'd find myself looking back on my day, puzzled at the fact that I didn't accomplish my goals.

The problem was I wasn't centered in Christ and aligning myself with His will. I allowed people and pressures to determine my day. Now, instead of responding to the various pulls, I've learned to intentionally seek Jesus, and every day shape my schedule around His purposes.

Richard Foster writes in his book *Longing for God*, "The goal of Scripture is to teach us to see the way our life fits into God's great story."[24] I love Foster's way of seeing life—we are invited into God's great story and each of us has a part to play. As we spend time with God, reading His Word, following His lead, and using our gifts, we begin to understand more clearly the role we were born to fill.

The apostle Paul said, "For to me, to live is Christ" (Phil. 1:21). I echo his passionate cry; therefore, I must choose to participate, to commit to, and to be company with people and events that further my ultimate purpose. Essentially, I must remember my life purpose gives me a filter through which I can determine my priorities.

For instance, because I want to:

Grow in my relationship with Jesus

Invest in people and activities that further His kingdom

Produce excellent work to the glory of God . . .

I must carefully choose and set my priorities. As I said before, a legacy doesn't just happen accidently.

> *Only one life,*
> *'Twill soon be past;*
> *Only what's done*
> *for Christ will last.*[25]

2. To Leave a Legacy We Must Live for Eternity

In his best-selling book *Crazy Love,* Francis Chan wrote, "Lukewarm people think about life on earth much more often than eternity in heaven. Daily life is mostly focused on today's to-do list, this week's schedule, and next month's vacation. Rarely, if ever, do they intently consider the life to come."[26] Regarding this, C. S. Lewis wrote, "If you read history you will find that the Christians who did the most for the present world were precisely those who thought most of the next. It is since Christians have largely ceased to think of the other world that they have become ineffective in this [one]."[27] This quote gives us another key that unlocks the door to leaving a legacy: a radiant woman must live for eternity.

As I ponder this truth, great men and women of the faith spring to mind. These men and women have one thing in common: they didn't live for the glory of this world but rather for the unfading glory of the next. As Paul wrote to the Corinthian church: *"Do you not know that in a race all the runners run, but only one gets the prize? . . . Everyone who competes in the games goes into strict training. They do it to get a crown that will not last; but we do it to get a crown that will last* **forever***"* (1 Cor. 9:24–25, emphasis added).

We must live with our eyes on the prize and with our gazes fixed on the finish line, leaving everything else behind. Only one thing matters, and it is the glory of God! We are living this life for that purpose, so when we see Jesus face-to-face, we can hear Him say, "Well done, my good and faithful servant." Radiant women should never be described as lukewarm. There's nothing warm about us—we are a blazing fire for the glory of God.

A recent conversation opened my eyes to a foundational problem that could pose as a stumbling block for those of us running the race in order to win the prize. Our culture has brainwashed many of us into believing that this world is all there is. Or rather, our culture has seduced us into believing that this world is better and our eternal destination is not nearly as sublime, cool, or desirable.

Whatever you do, don't buy into this lie! Eternity literally hangs in the balance.

No Worm Food

I had a realization while talking to a scruffy college student who I met on a flight from Sydney, Australia, to Los Angeles. To be honest, I always hope the seat next to me will remain empty, especially on flights that go into the double digits as this one did. Alas, my selfish desire was unmet because God had other plans.

"Scruffy" sat down next to me and from the start showed an air of friendliness. At least that was a bonus. I've sat next to grumpy businessmen way too many times. So, sitting next to a laid-back college guy for thirteen hours was a welcomed relief. He and I chatted a few minutes about Australia, and then spying my books, he asked, "What are you reading?" At this point in the flight, I knew I either would be in for a lengthy conversation, or he would politely beg the flight attendant for another seat. To my surprise, he wanted to talk.

I told him I was reading the Bible and a book about eternity. He gave me the polite, yet politically correct head nod that implied, "Who am I to judge?" Undeterred by the "Jesus Freak" label he placed upon me, he continued the conversation by asking, "So, you actually believe in eternity?"

Naively I said, "Of course. Don't you?"

"Oh, no, of course not. I'm way too evolved for that kind of thinking."

I was troubled by his use of the word *actually,* but he continued on with his explanation. He said, "We aren't immortal creatures with souls that will live for eternity. No, we are simply organisms with evolved prefrontal lobes that allow for emotions and cognitive thinking. Forget this silly notion that the human beings are eternal creatures and just face the fact: when we die, we just die. No heaven. No hell. Our sense of 'self' is absorbed back into the universe."

To which I replied, "Wow, your faith is truly amazing."

Puzzled, he said, "What do you mean by my 'faith'?"

I explained that I found it took extraordinary faith for someone to look at the universe, Earth, humanity, the complexity in the design of the atom, the sheer brilliance of DNA, and the absolute miracle of human life with thought, feelings, memory, abilities and a sense of purpose . . . and just chalk all of it up to mere chance.

He stared at me in perplexed silence.

At that point I was thinking, THANK YOU, JESUS for bringing that information to memory right when I needed it!

After pointing out the brilliance of God's design in creating Earth, I then turned my attention to mankind by considering the fact that sociologists have noted throughout human history every people group and society has instinctively held a belief in the afterlife and a higher power. As if a belief in eternity is literally hardwired into our DNA. Poor Scruffy thought he was dealing with a dumb blonde. He was not at all prepared when this Christian girl used physics, astronomy, logic, and sociology to prove that our faith is not blind or dumb but is very intelligent and capable of reason.

Don't get me wrong; this was not an argument but a very friendly conversation in which we both listened respectively to each other's worldviews. His worldview can be summarized as follows: there is not a creator; therefore, there is no purpose to this world or humanity. Humans are not souls who live for eternity. Because there is no god, how we live in this life does not matter. There is no explanation for the suffering and sadness, nor is there any hope for the future. Life just is.

On the other hand, a biblical worldview is the exact opposite: there is a Creator who purposed this world for His glory, and human beings are eternal creatures made in God's image with a magnificent calling and eternal destiny. This Creator has revealed Himself to man throughout history—through His prophets and ultimately in His Son. And all of the problems in this world—suffering, disease, hatred, war, crime—are the result of man's separation from God. But God made a way for relationship to be restored through the sacrificial death of His Son, Jesus.

At the end of our talk, he quietly said, "You've given me a lot to think about."

As he turned away to watch his in-flight movie, I thought to myself, *You've given me a lot to think about, too.*

What I've been pondering is how difficult it is for us to live for eternity when we are daily bombarded with messages that tell us to live it up because this world is all there is. When you die, you become worm food. Sorry for being a bit graphic, but isn't it true? Most of us were educated to dismiss the belief in a Creator, and consequently we were led to see this world apart from His work and eternal perspective.

Eternity is real. What we do with this life *does* matter. We can't allow the world to brainwash us into believing that nothing occurs when we die. To rightly reflect Jesus to the world, we must live in light of eternity.

Eternally Minded

I'm writing these words to Christians because even though we profess a biblical worldview sometimes the messages we hear sink into our thought lives and influence us subconsciously. For example, I recently watched the movie *The Bucket List,* a film about two men facing the last six months of their lives. Of course, the question arises of what happens after death. Jack Nicholson's character mocks anything that speaks of God and eternity. He summarizes his worldview with the statement, "We live. We die. And the wheels on the bus go round and round." Multiply that one line by the thousands we hear in the course of a lifetime, and it is so easy to see how it could chip away at our belief in eternity. Just as we discussed in previous chapters concerning our identities and purposes, we must be on guard against the subtle and not-so-subtle influences that shape our thinking and, consequently, our behavior.

I love what C. S. Lewis said about intentionally living for eternity in *Mere Christianity*: "I must keep alive in myself the desire for my true country, which I shall not find till after death; I must never let it get snowed under or turned aside; I must make it the main objective of life to press on to that other country and to help others do the same."[28] Yes, we must keep alive the desire and press on, for the world in which we live constantly distracts and tempts us to ignore the eternal and focus on the here and now.

This "new country," as Lewis described it, is our future eternal dwelling place with God. This book does not have space to describe the beauty, the wonder, the adventure, and the glory that awaits us. Yes, our lives will have purpose. No, we will not spend eternity floating on a cloud. God will create a new heaven and new earth where we will dwell with Him forever. No more crying, no more sorrow, no more pain. All things will be made new. Unblemished. Unspoiled. Unpolluted. Untainted by sin.

This new creation will be ours to enjoy with our Creator. Perhaps we will climb mountains, swim in the oceans, star gaze, ride horses through open pastures, and dance on fields of flowers. The Bible also teaches that we will rule and reign with Christ. Concerning this, Randy Alcorn writes, "God created Adam and Eve to be king and queen over the earth. Their job was to rule the earth, to the glory of God. They failed. Jesus Christ is the second Adam, and the church is his bride, the second Eve. Christ is king, the church is his queen. . . . God's saints will fulfill on the New Earth the role God first assigned to Adam and Eve on the old Earth."[29]

We will continually live out our designed purpose—glory. Oh, and how can I forget the feast? Yes, we shall feast! We are promised that, "No eye has seen, no ear has heard, no mind has conceived what God has prepared for those who love him" (1 Cor. 2:9; see also Isa. 64:4). Try as I may to describe it, I cannot. I just know that far better than my wildest imagination and far better than the best that Earth has to offer is just a foretaste of heaven.

Living for That Day

Where we spend eternity is determined by what we do with the cross of Jesus and His saving grace, but **how** we will live for eternity is determined by the way we live our lives here as believers.

Scripture is clear. Every human being will stand before God and give an account of his life. As Paul clearly states in Romans 14:10, 12, "we will all stand before God's judgment seat . . . each of us will give an account of himself to God." Those who reject Christ on Earth will be judged based on their works and will spend eternity separated from God in hell. I write these words with a heavy heart but at the same time know the most loving thing I can do for another human being is speak the truth—to urge them to receive God's gracious forgiveness and trust in Jesus.

The love of God is more than our minds can imagine. Even though we rebel and choose to turn away from our Source of Life, He still desires every person to be reconciled with Him and spend eternity in heaven. Yet the choice is ours. I love how Randy Alcorn describes God's goodness in his excellent book *Heaven*: "Consider the wonder of it: God determined that he would rather go to Hell on our behalf than live in Heaven without us. He so much wants us to *not* to go to Hell that he paid a horrible price on the cross that we wouldn't have to."[30]

Those who do trust in Christ and receive the free gift of grace are declared pardoned before God. When God looks at those who have trusted in Christ, instead of seeing our sin, He sees the perfection of Jesus. The judgment that awaits Christians is one that determines heavenly rewards. It is an evaluation of our lives on Earth. Because everything we have is a gift from God, we will be appraised based on how we used:

- Our time
- Our words
- Our talents
- Our treasure
- Our relationships

Did we use these to glorify God and further His kingdom, or did we put them to waste? How we live today matters for all eternity. Radiant women, let us not waste one more second, one more hour, or one more day. Let's run this race with eternity in view, and live for that day when each of us will stand before King Jesus.

Running the race brings to mind the Olympics. I live in a city where Olympic athletes from across the globe come to train in the area of track and field. I've had the privilege of observing them as I jog my humble laps at a nearby university's track. One thing I've noticed in these athletes is their fixed gaze. As they train, you can tell that their minds are somewhere else. What I've discovered is that they've learned to set their minds on the

Olympics. They imagine, with every practice sprint and hurdle, the moment they will race for gold.

Once again Paul teaches us the same principle when he encourages us to "Set your minds on things above, not on earthly things. . . . When Christ, who is your life, appears, then you also will appear with him in glory" (Col. 3:2, 4). How does living with eyes focused on eternity cause us to leave a lasting legacy? I think the answer is simple. When we live for eternity, we intentionally prioritize our lives around the things that matter the most to Jesus. What matters to Jesus? Jesus loves people, and He makes this clear in one of His final teachings while on earth. The way we treat people on this earth has eternal ramifications, not only for them but also for us.

> "When the Son of Man comes in his glory, and all the angels with him, he will sit on his throne in heavenly glory. All the nations will be gathered before him, and he will separate the people one from another as a shepherd separates the sheep from the goats. He will put the sheep on his right and the goats on his left.
>
> "Then the King will say to those on his right, 'Come, you who are blessed by my Father; take your inheritance, the kingdom prepared for you since the creation of the world. For I was hungry and you gave me something to eat, I was thirsty and you gave me something to drink, I was a stranger and you invited

me in, I needed clothes and you clothed me, I was sick and you looked after me, I was in prison and you came to visit me.'

"Then the righteous will answer him, 'Lord, when did we see you hungry and feed you, or thirsty and give you something to drink? When did we see you a stranger and invite you in, or needing clothes and clothe you? When did we see you sick or in prison and go to visit you?'

"The King will reply, 'I tell you the truth, whatever you did for one of the least of these brothers of mine, you did for me.'

"Then he will say to those on his left, 'Depart from me, you who are cursed, into the eternal fire prepared for the devil and his angels. For I was hungry and you gave me nothing to eat, I was thirsty and you gave me nothing to drink, I was a stranger and you did not invite me in, I needed clothes and you did not clothe me, I was sick and in prison and you did not look after me.'

"They also will answer, 'Lord, when did we see you hungry or thirsty or a stranger or needing clothes or sick or in prison, and did not help you?'

"He will reply, 'I tell you the truth, whatever you did not do for one of the least of these, you did not do for me.'

"Then they will go away to eternal punishment,
but the righteous to eternal life." (Matt. 25:31–46)

When we love Jesus, we love what He loves—people. His heart is one of mercy, compassion, generosity, and kindness. Those of us who are children of God are to be the hands and feet of Christ to a hurting world. Our job is to carry His love in word and deed to those we encounter. This is the work that leaves a legacy, and this is the very thing central to the heart of God.

Let me offer a word of caution. Remember, our power source is the Holy Spirit of God. God is the one who enables us to do the good works that bring Him glory (Eph. 2:8–10). The basis of our judgment as believers will be whether or not we are faithful in using the time, talents, and resources that God gives us. This includes our spiritual gifts.

The most important thing is that we intentionally love others with the love of Jesus. The remarkable truth is God even gives us the love that we need because in our natural state we don't love others. So, when we plug into our power source, are filled with the love of God, and are equipped by the Spirit of God, then our lives impact the world for all eternity. In doing so, the Bible tells us we lay up treasure in heaven.

I've often heard it said that there is no greater way to love someone than to assure that they will spend eternity with God. We do this by sharing with them the saving knowledge of Jesus Christ. Yet, so many of us have grown cold and apathetic about sharing our faith. I know it's cliché, but if you had the cure for cancer, wouldn't you shout it from the mountaintops and spend your life to eradicate the deadly disease?

Radiant women of God, think about the truth God has entrusted us with—His gospel message. Today you and I are His messengers to the world of the hope and healing available in Jesus Christ. If we are to leave a legacy, then we must be women passionate about leading others to Jesus.

3. To Leave a Legacy We Must Lead Others to Jesus

Bright lights.

Cameras rolling.

Producers shouting last-minute instructions.

The countdown begins: 10, 9, 8 . . . and then . . . the familiar music fills the room, and the famous (or infamous) Bob Barker takes the stage. On the edge of our seats, my college girlfriends and I were giddy with excitement.

We'd made it!!!

Months of planning and, finally, we were really there—live in the CBS television studio for the filming of *The Price Is Right*. A week in Los Angeles for spring break culminated with the three of us camping out at CBS in hopes of getting a seat in the audience for the show. Our sleep deprivation paid off!

With so much to absorb and take in, I was far too busy and preoccupied to listen when the producers gave instruction for the audience—us, the prospective contestants. Something about where to stand, blah, blah, what to do, blah, blah, blah . . . I wasn't listening. Alas, I was the proverbial "deer in headlights" when low and behold the first name called was MARIAN JORDAN . . . COME ON DOWN . . . YOU ARE THE FIRST CONTESTANT ON THE PRICE IS RIGHT!

Who?

Come on down?

What? Where? (insert: blank stare, dumb blonde look, frozen limbs, and friends hitting and shaking me into action)

And . . . . she's up!

I can't recall making it from my seat to the contestants' row down front. I do know that I didn't run screaming and waving my arms like I've seen other people do. I did more of a stumble forward, unsure-that-this-is-really-happening-to-me kind of movement—all the while trying not to get bulldozed by the overeager contestants now following close behind. It's all a haze.

Finally I reached my station. But before I could catch my breath, Bob (as we contestants like to call him) presented the first item up for bid: a Maytag refrigerator. Because I was the first contestant, it was up to me to start the bidding and give my estimation of the price.

It's all such a blur, but my PRICE was RIGHT!! The next thing I remember, I was on stage, kissed Bob Barker (on the cheek), and wondered, *Does the camera really add ten pounds, and if so did I wear the right jeans?* Once again I was not listening as Bob gave the instructions on how to play the game.

I'll spare you the humiliation of the next twelve minutes. I was a train wreck. Clueless. I didn't listen so I kept having to repeat the game until finally, only God knows how, I won! Yes, in spite of myself, I won the stinkin' game and moved on to SPIN THAT WHEEL!!!

This is where my glorious brush with fame ended—at the wheel. I didn't make it to the showcase showdown, but I did walk away that day with a new refrigerator, an all-expense paid trip to Boston, a recliner (or as I like to call it, the "Barker Lounger"), a lamp . . . and one fine story to tell.

That day—and a few days following—my excitement over winning was uncontainable. As we rushed from the CBS studios to LAX airport to catch our flight home, I told everyone I bumped into—including Robert Redford! Then, once I boarded the plane, I thought the flight attendant and other passengers needed to know the news. So I told them, and, of course, the minute I could get to my phone I called everyone I knew and shared my story of winning *The Price Is Right*.

All of this fuss over a silly game show.

What's funny to me is that, now, years later I rarely think about that experience. It's interesting how quickly my excitement faded and the enthusiasm fizzled. Today, most of my friends have no idea that I was even on the show. It's not something I talk about. It never comes up in conversation. Gone is the girl who couldn't wait to tell complete strangers and who was overflowing with excitement. Winning *The Price Is Right* is just a blip in my memory.

This fading passion reminds me of the fizzle that happens in the hearts of many Christians over sharing the miracle of salvation. At first, there is an overwhelming flood of emotion and a desire to share the newfound peace, hope, love, and joy with others. Yet, over time, we can grow numb, cold, and complacent. The emotional numbing leads to a lack of zeal for sharing the good news of Jesus with those whom we encounter.

Friends, let us not grow cold. Let us not forget the most amazing event that has ever occurred in human history. Let us not grow indifferent toward our salvation and cease sharing the amazing news: that God came to Earth to redeem us from the grip of sin.

Far greater than hearing the call to "come on down" on a silly game show, the God of the universe called us "out of darkness and into His marvelous light." Now, that's something to be excited about. But there's more! Forgiveness, freedom, healing, hope, security, love, acceptance, joy, peace, favor, blessings, wholeness, abundant life—the list of our "winnings" goes on and on.

So dear friends, wherever you are today, if you recognize apathy for the gospel in your own heart, please stop and pray, "Restore unto me the joy of Your salvation!" I understand. It's so easy to grow numb when we get busy with life and comfortable in our own salvation. But our passion quickly returns when we take an honest look at our sin, remember what Jesus rescued us from, and then humbly remember the price Jesus paid on the cross.

In order to win the battle over pride and apathy, we must remind ourselves daily that we deserve hell. We are not entitled to anything. God's grace is undeserved and came at a great price: the blood of Jesus Christ. A spirit of entitlement is the air we breathe in our culture. It is so difficult for us to remember that God doesn't owe us His love and mercy; it is a gift. When we stop and truly think about the cross of Jesus Christ and His sufferings *for us,* our hearts are filled anew with passion for His name.

Once again, the apostle Paul is a great role model. At the end of his life, his passion for Jesus and the gospel had not diminished one bit. His secret? Paul still saw himself as a sinner in need of grace. When we stop to remember how much we've been forgiven, our hearts will sing, "AMAZING GRACE! HOW SWEET THE SOUND THAT SAVED A WRETCH LIKE ME."

> And you, who were dead in your trespasses . . . God made alive together with him, having forgiven us all our trespasses, by cancelling the record of debt that stood against us with its legal demands. This he set aside, nailing it to the cross. (Col. 2:13 ESV)

When we keep in mind the amazing grace poured out on us, our hearts are stirred to share God's grace with others. Radiant women, *we* are His messengers, His ambassadors, and the proclaimers entrusted with the good news of salvation. He called you and me to go into all the world and preach the gospel (Matt. 28:19–20).[31]

Girlfriends, it's your time to shine. . . .

Go and Tell.

Live as Light.

Radiate Christ!

There is a world, lost in darkness, dying to know your Jesus.

SHINE ON!

Never forget, it's all about Jesus.
His Glory.
His Light.
His Radiance.

A radiant woman simply:
knows Him,
loves Him, and
lives to reflect Him to the world.

APPENDIX 1

The Work of the Holy Spirit

The Holy Spirit Convicts Us of Sin (John 16:8)

Jesus said, "When he comes, he will convict the world of guilt in regard to sin and righteousness and judgment."

As I write this section, I am praising God for this verse. Unless the Holy Spirit opens our eyes to see our sin, we never recognize our need for a Savior. It is God's mercy on us that His Spirit helps us to recognize our need for the cross.

I tell women all the time that conviction of sin is a gift. Without it, we would remain stuck and in bondage. But God, through His Spirit, makes us aware and causes us to come to repentance where we find grace and freedom!

The Holy Spirit Indwells Us (Rom. 8:9)

You, however, are controlled not by the sinful nature but by the Spirit, if the Spirit of God lives in you. And if anyone does not have the Spirit of Christ, he does not belong to Christ.

When we come to Jesus Christ by faith, we are born again (John 3). This new birth is by the Spirit, which produces in us a new nature—the life of Christ. Christ now lives within us by His Spirit.

The Holy Spirit Gives Us a New Heart with New Desires (Ezek. 36:26–27)

In foretelling the work of the Spirit, God prophesied: *"I will give you a new heart and put a new spirit within you; I will remove from you your heart of stone and give you a heart of flesh. And I will put My Spirit in you and move you to follow my decrees and be careful to keep my laws."*

This is one of my favorite Scriptures! I recall in my own life experiencing the transformation from a "heart of stone" that despised God and wanted to do my own will to the miracle of a "new heart" that loved God and longed to glorify Him. This miraculous transformation occurs by the Spirit of God working in our hearts and taking up residence. Now, with the Spirit living in us, we have both the desire and the power to live a life that glorifies God. He gives us radiance!

The Holy Spirit Helps Us in Our Weakness (Rom. 8:26)

The Spirit helps us in our weakness. We do not know what we ought to pray for, but the Spirit himself intercedes for us with groans that words cannot express.

Prayer is an expression of weakness, bringing us to God to acknowledge our dependence and need. In this place of weakness, the Holy Spirit intercedes for us, taking our pleas before the very throne of God.

The Holy Spirit Gives Us Understanding into God's Word (John 16:13)

Jesus said, "When he, the Spirit of truth, comes, he will guide you into all truth."

As believers, the Spirit of God helps us understand the Word of God. After all, He is the Author of Scripture. He gives us understanding and teaches us concerning Christ. As we read the Bible, we ask God to open our eyes to truth and to reveal His Son to us; it is the Spirit of God who makes the truth plain to us.

The Holy Spirit Speaks to Us (Acts 13:2)

While they were worshiping the Lord and fasting, the Holy Spirit said.

God speaks to us! The Holy One imparts wisdom, knowledge, direction, encouragement, truth, and comfort to His children. This is one of the greatest truths in the Bible. Jesus said, "My sheep listen to my voice" (John 10:27).

Yes, girls, we can know the voice of God. He does speak to us through His Word and in our hearts. He will never lead or guide us to do anything that dishonors God's name or contradicts His Holy character or His Word.

The Holy Spirit Produces a Love for God (Rom. 8:15–16 NIV)

You did not receive a spirit . . . [of] fear, but you received the Spirit of sonship. And by him we cry, "Abba, Father." The Spirit himself testifies with our spirit that we are God's children.

When we receive God's Spirit, we are born again as children of God. This produces in us a love for God. Now, we see God as "Abba"—Hebrew for "Daddy." Our whole mind-set toward God is one of love and affection.

The Holy Spirit Sanctifies (Transforming Us into the Likeness of Christ; 2 Thess. 2:13)

We ought always to thank God for you, brothers loved by the Lord, because from the beginning God chose you to be saved through the sanctifying work of the Spirit.

From the moment of our new birth, the Holy Spirit is at work in us to produce Christlike character. This transformation, called "sanctification," is the process in which we overcome the old sinful nature and become more like Christ, who is holy. It is important to remember that sanctification is a lifelong process. We participate in the process by surrendering to God's Spirit, studying His Word, praying, and daily remaining connected to Christ. Over time we will resemble the Radiant One, Jesus Christ, because of His Spirit's transforming power in us.

The Holy Spirit Produces Christ's Character (Fruit; Gal. 5:22–23)

The fruit of the Spirit is love, joy, peace, patience, kindness, goodness, faithfulness, gentleness and self-control.

I believe this is one of the most misunderstood and misapplied Scriptures in the whole Bible. So often you will hear teachers say, "A Christian should strive to be loving or joyful." Yet, the truth is that we cannot change in our own power.

We need Jesus and His Spirit living in us to produce godly character. The fruit of the Spirit is the evidence that someone is controlled by God's Spirit. For instance, an apple tree doesn't strive or strain to produce apples. No, the result of its nature is apple production. Likewise, when we are indwelled and filled with God's Spirit, then the natural "produce" of our lives is His character (or fruit).

The Holy Spirit Equips Us with Spiritual Gifts (1 Cor. 12:4–7)

There are different kinds of gifts, but the same Spirit. There are different kinds of service, but the same Lord. There are different kinds of working, but the same God works all of them in all men. Now to each one the manifestation of the Spirit is given for the common good.

Every believer is equipped with gifts of the Spirit to use for the glory of God. The purpose of these gifts is to testify of Christ and to build up the church. Every one of us is empowered for service in God's kingdom. You have a special role to play in glorifying His name. Don't hide your gifts—let them shine!

APPENDIX 2

Small Group Questions

Chapter One

1. Marian uses the example of a bride on her wedding day to illustrate radiance. Describe a bride that you've seen who was truly radiant. Why was she glowing?

2. Marian writes: *"Brides are most often described as radiant for a very good reason. It is universally acknowledged that a woman is most beautiful when she is in love. When basking in the glow of another's love, she feels whole, complete, confident, and adored; her outer expression and countenance emanate from an inner reality. She knows she is loved, and she is head over heels in love with her groom. That, my friends, is radiance."*

Not all of us have been brides, but describe a time when you've felt radiant (glowing from within).

3. What motivated Mary Magdalene to rush to the empty tomb on Easter Sunday? What touched you about her story?

4. Marian writes: *"Like Mary, I fell head over heels in love with my Savior. How could I not? Forgiveness fuels love's flame. I was whole and healed, something I'd never known before Him. This love drove me, propelled me, to follow after Jesus with my whole heart. And I did. The more I followed Him, the more I loved Him. The more He revealed Himself to me through His Word, the more my life was transformed for His glory. I, too, was enthralled. I couldn't wait to spend time with Him. I was ruined for anything else but Jesus."*

Have you experienced this type of heart transformation? If yes, describe it. If no, do you want to? What did Marian say was the key to this transformation?

5. According to this chapter, why is our love for God a "battlefield"?

6. What is a radiant woman's motivation for living a pure and holy life?

7. Read Matthew 5:14. Who in your life would you describe as a radiant woman . . . a light in the darkness?

Chapter Two

1. Marian uses the movie *My Fair Lady* as an illustration of transformation. What other movie or story also illustrates this truth.

2. Marian writes: *"The word* redemption *means to 'buy something back and to restore it to its original intent.' Every human heart beats to be redeemed, restored to our original intention. Instinctively, we know that we were created for more. We were indeed created for glory, formed to manifest radiance. Christianity is the ultimate transformation story. You and I are invited into a relationship with God, and in this relationship we are transformed from the inside out—from darkness to light. Jesus takes our brokenness and forms something beautiful. We are transformed into a masterpiece for which only He could get the glory. Miraculously, sinners become saints, the lost are found, and the blind can see."*

Read the following Scripture passages to discover more about redemption:

1 Peter 1:18–19

1 Peter 2:9–10

Ephesians 1:7

Colossians 1:13–14

3. Why is authentic transformation so vital?

4. Why was Moses radiant? What caused him to glow? What do we learn from his experience?

5. Read section entitled "Son-Kissed Glow." Describe a time when your love for Christ propelled you to share His love with

others. Describe a time when you missed an opportunity to do so.

Jesus said that His followers are "the light of the world." What do you think would happen if you and your friends took up the charge to live as light in the darkness? What would you need to do? What would you stop doing? Who would you treat differently?

Chapter Three

1. Marian opens this chapter with a story about a forgotten ID. Share a time when you forgot something extremely important.

2. Read section entitled "Identity in Christ." What is our identity in Christ? Why is it important?

3. What does Marian mean by the statement "We behave how we believe"? How does her pig story illustrate this truth?

4. Marian writes: *"Before I met Jesus, my identity was formed primarily by my culture and my experiences. My culture shaped me in many ways (through movies, television, and education) into its mold. From this mold emerged a woman who lived for people's approval, feared rejection, hated her body, lived a dangerous and promiscuous lifestyle, and believed her worth was found in gaining a guy's attention. My culture convinced me that my ID read 'usable object.'"*

What other IDs does our culture place upon women?

5. In what ways do women today strive to feel "chosen and

loved"? Marian writes: *"You are chosen and loved by God. This is not something you can earn. This is who you are."* How does believing this truth transform a woman?

6. How does the movie *Taken* depict God's love for us?

7. What does it mean when Scripture says that we are "members of the royal priesthood"?

8. The word *holy* means "set apart." Marian describes holiness as living as God's precious treasure. She writes: *"Like my expensive teacup, God sees you and me as His treasure. That's what holiness is about. Living a life that reflects your value. Refusing to devalue what was worth dying for."*

How would you respond to the question Marian asks in this section? Do you treat yourself as holy? And do you expect others to do the same?

9. Based on this chapter, why is remembering your identity in Christ essential to living a radiant life?

Chapter Four

1. Do you ever feel discouraged about your relationship with God? Do you ever feel like a failure at some aspect of the Christian life? Do you ever feel like your light is dim? If yes, explain why.

2. What did Marian's Texas star illustration explain about a Christian's relationship with the Holy Spirit?

3. Why is it impossible for us to be the light of the world in our own power?

4. Explain the phrase "whatever fills us, controls us." What does this chapter teach about the power of the Spirit?

5. Marian describes two "radiant barriers" in this chapter. Name each and give a short description.

6. Which radiant barrier is presently blocking God's light in you?

7. Read the following excerpt and discuss:

"When the Spirit of God comes to dwell in us, we have a new nature and a new desire. We want Jesus to be applauded, lifted up, and exalted. He is the Famous One whose praise we live to proclaim. Of course, there is a battle between our old sinful nature and the Spirit of God living in us; but each time we say yes to the Spirit, we overcome the flesh—fulfilling our purpose of glorifying God.

"The Holy Spirit will always shine the spotlight on Jesus. This serves as a good litmus test for our lives. We can know if we are under the Spirit's influence by whether or not our lives are bringing Jesus glory."

Chapter Five

1. Looking back over the various fashion trends that have come and gone, name a time when you were a fashion victim.

2. How does a person's wardrobe express their identity?

3. Read Romans 13:11–14 and discuss the following excerpt from this chapter.

"One thing I'd like to clarify from the start is why we undergo this wardrobe change. It is not an attempt to earn our salvation or to make us acceptable before God. Actually, it is the opposite. The reason we change our clothes is because we are now different people, new creations in Christ—complete with new clothing that reflects this new identity."

4. What are a few things that a Christian woman should "take off" and "put on" if she desires to live a radiant life?

5. What does it mean to "make no provision for the flesh"?

6. Marian proposes two reasons why Christians today aren't more loving. What are these reasons? (Hint: they both begin with the letter B.)

7. Read Ephesians 4:22–27, 29. What should a radiant woman put off? Share an example of how words can harm or hurt others.

8. Explain the phrase "clothe yourself in humility." How is pride the opposite of radiance?

9. Read the following excerpt and discuss.

"Before someone mistakenly assumes that humility then means low self-esteem, let me quickly say, 'No.' Humility, as C. S. Lewis said, 'is not thinking less of yourself, it is thinking of yourself less.' I hope you can discern the difference. When God is in His rightful place in our hearts, then we see ourselves rightly: sinners in need of grace who are redeemed by the precious blood of Jesus. We recognize our true value and worth in Him, but at the same time, this truth humbles us."

Chapter Six

1. In this chapter Marian shares a story of a divided heart. How would you feel if you were in her shoes? How do you think God feels when our hearts are divided?

2. Marian writes: *"our ex is the world system that Jesus Christ redeemed us from when we placed our faith in Him. James Boice describes the world as 'an organized system, made up of a set of ideas, people, activities, purposes, used by Satan for opposing the work of Christ on earth. It is the very opposite of what is godly.' It is that very kingdom of darkness Boice describes that held us captive before Jesus rescued us, bringing us into the 'kingdom of light'"* (Col. 1:12–13).

Share examples of how you've felt pulled back into the world.

What temptations do you face that you recognize as lures from your ex?

3. Marian writes: *"Every woman must ask herself, 'Am I influencing the world, or is the world influencing me?'"*

How would you honestly answer this question? Are you shining as a light or is the darkness hiding your glow?

4. What can a radiant woman take away from the Samson and Delilah story?

5. What are the three warning signs of a divided heart?

6. In this chapter, Marian highlighted several ways that media can "brainwash" us into the world's mode of thinking

and behaving. What influencer has impacted you the most and why?

7. How does materialism cause a divided heart?

8. How does Solomon's story of a divided heart caution us today?

Chapter Seven

1. What is a legacy? Whose life has impacted your own in a similar way as Jill's did to Marian?

2. What does the apostle Paul teach us about leaving a legacy?

3. Marian shares three essentials needed to intentionally pursue Jesus. What are these essentials?

4. What role does prayer play in the radiant Christian life?

5. What priority does God's Word play in your life? What changes do you need to implement in your daily routine in order to spend time daily in God's Word?

6. Marian writes: *"Radiant women, it is time for us to rise up!!! We cannot fall into the cultural traps of apathy and laziness, or even the busyness that can take us away from prioritizing Christ. We cannot waste our lives, missing out on the high calling that God has for each one of us.*

"Yes, I'm talking to you. You are called of God. You have a part to play in His kingdom. You are extremely significant in God's purposes. If all of us don't wake up, seize the day, and align our

lives with God's will, we will get to the end of our lives and have very little to show for it."

What is your response to this encouragement?

7. How does living for eternity cause us to shine brighter in the midst of darkness here and now?

8. According to Matthew 25:31–46, does God care how we spend our time on Earth? Will it matter in eternity?

9. Marian writes: *"Radiant women of God, think about the truth God has entrusted us with—His gospel message. Today, you and I are His messengers to the world of the hope and healing available in Jesus Christ. If we are to leave a legacy, then we must be women passionate about leading others to Jesus."*

Who has God placed in your path who needs to know Jesus?

10. What did Marian's story about *The Price Is Right* caution against? What is the key to maintaining passion?

Acknowledgments

I owe a huge debt of gratitude to so many for their faithful prayers, support, and contributions to *Radiant*. First of all, I want to thank the women of Second Baptist Church in Houston who first participated in the *Radiance* Bible study. I'm forever grateful for our time studying the Word and digging into these topics together.

To the board of directors of Redeemed Girl Ministries: Anita, Kitty, Tonya, Matt and Jessica, Jeff and Jenny, Ryan and Kim, Leti and Chaz, Leigh, and Susannah. You guys are the best! I am overwhelmed with gratitude as I think of the support you provide. Heaven alone knows the mountains that your prayers have moved!

I'm especially thankful for Angel Texada and Catherine King. Truly, I can't imagine a better creative and editorial team. Thank you for serving God with your amazing gifts and sacrificially giving of your time.

To the wonderful team at B&H Publishing: I'm so blessed to work with individuals who passionately love Jesus and who desire for women to know Him.

Lauren. I simply can't imagine how I ever did ministry without you. I'm so proud of the woman of God that you are and how you truly shine for Jesus. Thank you for listening to every word of this book, multiple times, as you were patiently trying to focus on something else. And for the emergency Starbucks and Sonic drinks to keep me going . . . you are the best!

To my incredible family, I love you guys so much! I am grateful for the grace you've extended to me and the love you poured out on me even when I was at times far from radiant.

Finally, to my Jesus, You are the Light of the world. Thank You for rescuing me from darkness! Thank You for life and for the joy of serving in Your kingdom. Apart from You I can do nothing!

Notes

1. The Newsboys, *Shine* (New Kensington, PA: Whitaker House, 2002), 49.

2. *Webster's Ninth New Collegiate Dictionary*, S.V. "Thirst."

3. Sinclair B. Ferguson, *The Holy Spirit: Contours of Christian Theology* (Downers Grove: InterVarsity Press, 1996), 91–92.

4. Dr. Henry Cloud and Dr. John Townsend, *How People Grow* (Grand Rapids: Zondervan, 2004), 104.

5. Nancy Leigh DeMoss, *Seeking Him* (Chicago: Moody Publishers, 2009), used by permission by Revive Our Heart Ministries.

6. Remember, when indwelled by God's Spirit we have the very nature of Christ. He makes us holy by perfectly meeting God's standard. Now, we are living out of God's power, not our old sinful nature.

7. For more information about God's design for sex, visit www.redeemedgirl.org or read my book *Sex and the City Uncovered*.

8. Leanne Payne, *Listening Prayer* (Grand Rapids: Baker Books, 1999), 48.

9. Repent means to change from pursuing or committing a sinful action to instead pursue God's will for how you should act in that area of your life.

10. Tim Keller, "The Advent of Humility," Jesus is the reason to stop concentrating on ourselves, http://www.christianitytoday.com/ct/2008/december/20.51.html.

11. James Montgomery Boice, *The Epistles of John: An Expositional Commentary* (Grand Rapids: Baker Books, 2006).

12. C. J. Mahaney, *Worldliness: Resisting the Seduction of a Fallen World* (Wheaton: Crossway Books, 2008), 42.

13. Ibid., 40.

14. Ibid., 93.

15. Ibid., 95–96.

16. See http://www.hymnsite.com/lyrics/umh400.sht "Come, Thou Fount of Every Blessing"; text, Robert Robinson, 1735–90.

17. Kenneth W. Osbeck, *52 Hymn Stories Dramatized* (Grand Rapids, MI: Krogel Publications, 1992).

18. George MacDonald, *Ordering Your Private World* (Nashville: Thomas Nelson, 1984), 145.

19. Ibid., 146.

20. For more teaching on prayer and prayer resources, visit www.redeemedgirl.org.

21. MacDonald, *Ordering Your Private World*, 140.

22. Gary Thomas, *Holy Available* (Grand Rapids: Zondervan, 2009), 224.

23. MacDonald, *Ordering Your Private World*, 72.

24. Richard J. Foster and Gayle D. Beebe, *Longing for God* (Downers Grove: IVP Books, 2009), 52.

25. John Piper, *Don't Waste Your Life* (Wheaton: Crossway Books, 2010).

26. Francis Chan, *Crazy Love: Overwhelmed by a Relentless God* (Colorado Springs: David C. Cook), 75.

27. C. S. Lewis, *Mere Christianity* (New York: Collier Books, 1960, 118.

28. C. S. Lewis, *Mere Christianity* (New York: HarperCollins, 2001), 137.

29. Randy Alcorn, *Heaven* (Carol Streams, IL: Tyndale House Publishers, 2004), 215.

30. Ibid., 28.

MORE BOOKS BY
MARIAN JORDAN